NEIL T. ANDERSON

WINNING
THE
BATTLE
WITHIN

HARVEST HOUSE PUBLISHERS

EUGENE, OREGON

Cover by Dugan Design Group, Bloomington, Minnesota

Harvest House Publishers is the exclusive licensee of the trademark, THE BONDAGE BREAKER.

The names of certain persons mentioned in this book have been changed in order to protect the privacy of the individuals involved.

WINNING THE BATTLE WITHIN
Expanded and updated from *Finding Freedom in a Sex-Obsessed World*
Copyright © 2004/2008 by Neil T. Anderson
Published by Harvest House Publishers
Eugene, Oregon 97402
www.harvesthousepublishers.com

ISBN-13: 978-0-7369-2422-1

Library of Congress Cataloging-in-Publication Data
Anderson, Neil T., 1942-
Winning the battle within / Neil T. Anderson.—[Updated & expanded ed.].
p. cm.
Rev. ed. of: Finding freedom in a sex-obsessed world. 2004.
Includes bibliographical references.
ISBN-13: 978-0-7369-1298-3

1. Chastity. 2. Sex—Religious aspects—Christianity. 3. Lust—Religious aspects—Christianity. I. Anderson, Neil T., 1942- Finding freedom in a sex-obsessed world. II. Title.
BV4647.C5A557 2008
241'.66—dc22

2008001010

Printed in the United States of America
09 10 11 12 13 14 15 16 / VP-SK / 11 10 9 8 7 6 5 4 3 2

To my wife, Joanne

You are my helpmate, best friend, and confidante.
I love you.

Acknowledgments

You are to be commended for picking up this book. It shows you have the courage to face the truth with a desire to find your freedom in Christ, or the freedom of someone you love.

The time it took to write this book was but a fraction of the time I have spent with hurting Christians. Many have been victims of sexual abuse, and others have been carried away by lustful fantasies, enticed by a world spiraling out of control into a cesspool of sexual madness. Many of the abused have become abusers. They have all borne the shame of a defiled temple and cringed under the accusations of the evil one. They are your sons and daughters, spouses, friends, and co-workers. If you heard their stories, you would weep with them.

I want to thank my friend, Dr. Charles Mylander, for reading this manuscript and writing the foreword. The editorial staff at Harvest House Publishers has always been a delight to work with. You have helped me be a better writer.

Finally, I want to thank my wife, Joanne, who reads all my manuscripts, and to whom I have dedicated this book.

CONTENTS

FOR THOSE WHO
ARE STRUGGLING

I wish this powerful book had been mine when I was going through my own savage struggle with lustful thoughts. For years they plagued my mind and irritated my soul. I tried everything I thought a Christian should try—Bible study and memorization, new experiences with God, and efforts at self-discipline—but nothing seemed to work for long.

I prayed during those times of struggle, too—God knows I prayed. I repented and turned away from my sins more often than I can remember. God answered my prayers at the moment. But the lustful thoughts always came back. Although I did not fall into an adulterous affair and avoided pornography like the plague, lust was the battleground of my Christian experience. I took three steps forward and two steps back, then two steps forward and three steps back, and then one step forward and four steps back.

Yes, there were holy-ground moments of fresh victory before God. I loved them. But then came the agonizing weeks and months of defeat. I hated them and hated my sin, yet I could not escape it. What Paul describes in Romans 7 describes my experience perfectly. I studied the message of Romans 6 through 8 and tried to apply it. Somehow it worked in every area of my life except one. I could not seem to live constantly in the Spirit when it came to lust. There was something compulsive about my thought life that felt abnormal to me. Little did I know how real the spiritual problem truly was.

During these years of silent, hidden struggle I felt I had no one to talk to. Later I figured out that there was no one I *wanted* to talk to. My pride and my shame almost did me in. I described my turning point in my book *Running the Red Lights.* That turning point was effective in setting me free in Christ, but now I know it was unnecessary for me to have waited so long.

This book's biblical insight based on Paul's teaching in the Roman epistle of renouncing every sexual use of my body and mind outside of marriage proved so helpful when I first heard it. My temptations were much more normal by that time, and the compulsiveness was already broken. Nevertheless, as I asked Christ to bring to my mind each instance of sexual sin, three vivid memories popped into my thoughts. Each one was, I now believe, a foothold Satan used to form a stronghold in my mind. Renouncing each one led to greater freedom and joy than ever before.

In the days of my greatest struggle I did not know about the activity of Satan in putting his evil thoughts in my mind. I did not know my true identity as a man who was crucified, buried, made alive, raised up, and seated with Christ (Galatians 2:20; Romans 6:4; Ephesians 2:4-6). I did not know how to apply God's grace and truth to take every thought captive in obedience to Christ. I did not understand the spiritual authority over the evil one that is mine in Christ, which is so powerfully taught by Dr. Anderson. The Lord did teach me many lessons about becoming a winner and overcoming the lust of the flesh, but if I had had this book back then and understood the spiritual battle I was in, Christ would have set me free years sooner.

Most Christians desperately need this message, either for their present struggle or for something in their past that has not been resolved. Any good Christian book is like a cherry pie. Some readers will always find a pit that doesn't fit their theological grid and then be tempted to throw away the whole pie. Please don't do that. The message of this book has the potential to show millions of people how Christ can set them free from sexual bondage. Read it, pass it on, and spread the word.

Dr. Charles Mylander
Executive Director of Evangelical Friends Mission

YOU CAN
EXPERIENCE
FREEDOM

On November 21, 2003, I was watching the Sunday evening television program *60 Minutes*. One segment was on "Adult Entertainment," which I didn't particularly care to watch, but I ended up downloading a hard copy of the news report because I was so astonished by what they said. In summary:

- $10,000,000,000 is spent every year on adult entertainment, and "reputable" industries like General Motors, Marriott Hotels, and Time Warner are cashing in because the profit margin is so high.

- There are 800 million adult videotapes and DVDs in video stores available for rent.

- In 2002, the porn industry produced 11,000 video titles.

- The porn industry employs 12,000 people in California alone.

- Among the guests at major hotels, 50 percent will use pay-per-view porn, which accounts for 75 percent of the hotels' video profits.

- Type in the word *sex* in an Internet search engine like Google and you will get over 900 million results. In the period from 2003 to 2008 that number tripled!

The program showed video clips of sex conventions held in civic centers, and the reporters interviewed scores of singles and married couples who were looking for the ultimate experience of sexual stimulation. The only person on the show who was speaking out against the industry was a female United States representative who was trying to introduce legislation to ensure that the female "actresses" were not being abused. In other words, almost every form of adult "entertainment" is legal, and it is a huge business.

A report from the Centers for Disease Control from the year 2000 (now eight years ago!) tells us that

> in the United States, more than 65 million people are currently living with an incurable sexually transmitted disease (STD). An additional 15 million people become infected with one or more STDs each year, roughly half of whom contract life-long infections (Cates, 1999).

Dave Foster, the child of a Presbyterian pastor, gained some fame as an actor. He wasn't acting when he doubled as a male prostitute. Life in the gutter finally drove him to Christ, and he has become a powerful witness for sexual freedom and healing through his ministry, Mastering Life Ministries. According to David, out of sixteen people sitting in a pew in any church, two will be struggling with sexual identity. He is not suggesting that one in eight is gay—he is saying that one in eight has some mental confusion about their sexual orientation.

Further, four of the sixteen people are sexual-abuse victims. The "official" estimate is that

NO DEAL

I surveyed the student body of a good conservative seminary and found that 60 percent of the male student body was presently feeling some sexual guilt. Out of that group, 50 percent said they would take an elective that would train and help students and others overcome sexual bondage for credit, if it were offered. Would you care to guess what happened when I showed these results to the dean?

one out of every four women and one out of every seven men is a victim, but that is based only on what is reported, which makes the more likely scenario to be one out of every three women and one out of every four men. In the same pew of sixteen people, an additional four will struggle with some form of sexual addiction, and that is true of every pew in your church. Those numbers would also hold true if every person sitting in the pew were a pastor, every one of whom are human beings just like the rest of us.

But There Is Hope

Rick's life was an endless quest for acceptance, significance, and intimacy with those who would accept him. As a child, he was sexually abused by his grandmother after his father committed suicide. As a young man, he embarked on a desperate search to fill the void in his life. After marrying his college sweetheart, Emily, he kept trying to cover his bitterness and pain with extramarital sexual encounters, excessive work, and the approval of others—but to no avail. Emily lost patience with him and left.

While listening to a tape by Dr. Charles Stanley, Rick fell to his knees and asked Jesus to save him from himself and from the sin that never delivered what it promised. He and his wife were reconciled, and together they bore four children. To others they appeared to be a respectable Christian family.

Rick, however, was still haunted by the lies that his needs for acceptance, security, and significance could somehow be met by satisfying his lusts for sex, food, social acceptance, and affirmation at work. He fell back into his old patterns of immorality. He was sexually involved with numerous partners, including a married woman, while continuing to play the role of the Christian husband and father. His double life left his soul in turmoil.

Devastated by the breakup of an affair, Rick confessed everything to his family and entered a three-month inpatient program for his addictions. Emily was crushed and told him not to return home. The divorce that followed prompted Rick to make an attempt at renewing his faith in Christ. He prayed and committed himself to not get involved sexually during his 90 days of treatment. His continuing belief that the right woman would meet his deep and seemingly unquench-able need for love only led to more failure. While he continued doing daily devotions, seeking God's guidance, and "witnessing" to his co-workers, he was involved with yet another married woman.

Rick rode a spiritual and emotional roller coaster. His convictions would drive him to break off relationships and return to the Lord. Then personal problems and depression would lead him back to the same old flesh patterns of sex and food. Rick explains his futile attempts to control his behavior:

> The "pimp" in my mind repeatedly promised me fulfillment if I would only prostitute myself one more time. But the lies never fulfilled their promises. Life for me was like pushing a car. When things were going all right, it required only a little effort. But every time I tried to push the car over the mountain of my sexual bondage, the car rolled back over me—leaving me desperate, hurt, and hopeless. I couldn't stop this cycle no matter how much I sought God. My sexual addiction ruled everything in my life. I hated it, I knew it was destroying me from the inside out—but I kept heeding the pimp in my mind again and again.

Rick's godly mother encouraged him to attend my "Living Free in Christ" conference. During the first evening of the conference he was harassed by sexual fantasies in his mind. However, he did hear one statement that gave him some hope: "If the Son sets you free, you will be free indeed" (John 8:36). Rick said, "I knew I wasn't free. I was powerless to stop the fruitless search for fulfillment and satisfaction in sex, food, and work."

He made an appointment to meet with me privately during the conference and shared his testimony as follows:

> I knew while driving to the meeting that something was going to happen. My heart felt like it was going to explode. There was a war raging within me. The pimp in my mind,

who had controlled my life for years, didn't want me to go. But I was determined to experience the freedom Neil talked about.

I expected Neil to slap me on the side of the head and shout out an exorcistic prayer. Then I would surely fall to the floor and flop around uncontrollably until the effects of his prayer set me free. It didn't happen that way. Neil listened quietly as I shared my story, then he said in a calm voice, "Rick, you can be free in Christ."

As Neil led me through the Steps to Freedom in Christ, I could hear the pimp's insistent lies in my mind. The inner battle was intense, but I was ready for the shackles to be broken. So I repented of my sin, renounced all the lies I had believed, renounced every sexual use of my body as an instrument of unrighteousness, and forgave all those who had offended me. As I did, peace began to roll in and drown out 37 years' worth of lies. I sensed a holy silence in my mind. The pimp was gone and, praise God, I was free!

Rick's freedom was tested right away. The next day during the conference he was bombarded by immoral thoughts. But he took those thoughts captive to the obedience of Christ and chose to believe the truth that he was a child of God, alive and free in Christ. That night he was tempted to pursue another destructive relationship. He called upon the Lord, and the "holy silence" returned.

Rick has since experienced a genuine and growing relationship with his heavenly Father. He stopped watching the raunchy television programs and movies that played a large part in feeding his lustful habits. His newfound freedom in Christ resulted in a desire to study the Bible and pray, which before were tiresome religious duties to be performed.

Every Child of God Can Find Their Freedom in Christ

Every child of God in sexual bondage, and those who have been sexually exploited by others, can experience their freedom in Christ through genuine repentance and faith in God. Only then can they continue in the process of being conformed to the image of God. Jesus broke the power of sin on the cross and defeated the devil. Because of His resurrection we can have new life in Him and be set free from our past so we can be all He created us to be. This truth can be appropriated by anyone who puts their trust in God and genuinely repents of their sins.

Secular treatment centers and a myriad of self-help programs offered Rick no success resolving his sexual addiction, which was bundled together with his early childhood experiences and every other aspect of his life. For him, sexual promiscuity was a self-gratifying attempt to be somebody. All attempts to seek self-verification through appearance, performance, and social status in this fallen world will fail. We can be complete only in Christ (Colossians 1:28).

Christianity, when properly understood, offers the only truly wholistic answer, which is essential for complete resolution of our problems. The solution is never a single-focused one, because people don't have sex problems, or alcohol problems, or marriage problems—they have *life* problems, which are inextricably bound up in our relationships with God, family, friends, neighbors, and co-workers. Sex is not just a physical phenomenon—it is integrally related to the body, soul, and spirit.

I shared Rick's story because I wanted to expose the spiritual side of his problem, which primarily manifests itself as a battle for the mind. Secular treatment centers are not going to address that, and many Christian recovery ministries don't either. Complete recovery begins by submitting to God, but it will remain incomplete without resisting the devil (James 4:7). The enemies of our sanctification are the world, the flesh, and the devil. Trying to separate the psychological from the spiritual creates a false dichotomy. Our problems are never *not* psychological, and they are never *not* spiritual. God is a Spirit, and He "upholds all things by the word of His power" (Hebrews 1:3 NASB). Sexual bondage is a body, soul, and spirit problem that requires a body, soul, and spirit answer, as do all other mental and emotional problems.

It is important to clarify that I did not set Rick free. Nor did the

Steps to Freedom in Christ, which are just a tool that gives structure to the repentance process of helping people submit to God and resist the devil. Knowing the truth, followed by genuine repentance, is *what* set Rick free. *Who* set Rick free was Jesus, and He is the only one who can set captives free and bind up the brokenhearted. Rick is not a sexual pervert, adulterer, or fornicator—he is a child of God, a joint heir with Jesus, and a new creation in Christ. Knowing his identity and position in Christ is what enables him to live a righteous life by faith in the power of the Holy Spirit.

Learning to Experience Your Freedom

In this book I will consider our sexuality in light of God's original plan in creation, then discuss the effects of the fall and how sin perverts our character and understanding. I will then look at some Old Testament guidelines for sexual purity and marriage and explain why nobody could live a righteous life under the law. I will use the story of David to illustrate the downward spiral to sexual bondage. Finally, we will discuss God's answer for sexual freedom and purity under the New Covenant of grace. Every child of God is alive and free in Christ, and every one of us can experience our freedom if we know the truth and are willing to repent.

The conclusion of the book offers an opportunity to go through the Steps to Freedom in Christ. You can process this book and the Steps on your own—however, I am designing the book so it can be used for small-group study. I have included discussion questions at the end of each chapter for this purpose. They are not intended to reveal anyone's personal sins. I would further suggest that men and women meet in separate groups because of the sensitive nature of the subject. This should also make it easier for participants to share and ask questions.

The seminary I mentioned earlier offered no elective to help its students. Many pastors and Christian leaders reading this book will be tempted to do nothing as well, and at least half the people sitting in those church pews will continue to struggle. If your church won't offer this opportunity, why don't you gather some like-minded men and women and say, "Let's go through this together."

It is never my intention to embarrass anybody, or add to their guilt. Guilt and shame are counterproductive to recovery. I will explain how an individual or group can go through the Steps to Freedom without embarrassing anyone. This repentance process will also resolve a lot of other mental and emotional problems as well, such as depression, anxiety, fear, and anger. It pains me to think how many people are living in bondage to sin, when I know that Jesus came to set them free. I pray that this book will make some small contribution to that end.

Neil T. Anderson

PART ONE

1

TROUBLE IN THE GARDEN

Human sexuality is too noble and beautiful a thing, too profound a form of experience, to turn into a mere technique or physical relief, or a foolish and irrelevant pastime.

J.V.L. CASSERLEY

I was asked to speak at a community college on the topic of sexuality from a Christian perspective. There were about 25 students in attendance, and all but three were women. One young man had pulled his desk into the corner at the front of the class, and he read a paper while I was talking. If I said anything he didn't agree with, he showed his disapproval with a loud "raspberry." In the question-and-answer session, a woman asked what Christians teach about masturbation. Before I could answer, he said so all could hear, "Well, I do it every day!"

"Congratulations," I said. "Can you stop?" There were no more raspberries or comments from him for the rest of the class. He was the last to leave and remarked on the way out, "Why would I want to stop?" "That is not what I asked you," I said, and I continued by saying, "What you think is freedom, I think is bondage, and you will discover that the moment you try to stop."

The secular world has little knowledge of what God created to be good. Unfortunately, most of what the world hears from the church is what the church is against, and they delight in pointing out our failures to live up to our own prohibitions.

⊹⊱═◎═⊰⊹

God revealed His plan for the sexual life and health of humanity in the creation account recorded in Genesis 2:18,21-25:

> The LORD God said, "It is not good for the man to be alone. I will make a helper suitable for him."...So the LORD God caused the man to fall into a deep sleep; and while he was sleeping, he took one of the man's ribs and closed up the place with flesh. Then the LORD God made a woman from the rib he had taken out of the man, and he brought her to the man.
>
> The man said, "This is now bone of my bones and flesh of my flesh; she shall be called 'woman,' for she was taken out of man." For this reason a man will leave his father and mother and be united to his wife, and they will become one flesh.
>
> The man and his wife were both naked, and they felt no shame.

God created Adam in His own image and breathed life into him, and Adam became spiritually and physically alive. Something was missing, however. It wasn't good for Adam to be alone—he needed a suitable helpmate. None of the animals God had created could provide a complementary relationship with him. So God created Eve from Adam's rib. Male and female He created them. They were sexual beings from the beginning.

The first couple were naked and unashamed. There were no dirty or offensive parts of their body. Intimate sexual relationships were not separate from their relationship with God, and their union was fully consummated in the presence of God. There was no sin, and there was nothing to hide. Adam and Eve had no reason to cover up their nakedness.

Their purpose and responsibility was to "be fruitful and increase in number; fill the earth and subdue it" (Genesis 1:28). Sex was intended for procreation as well as pleasure. They didn't "make" love. Sexual intercourse and physical touch were the means by which the two could express their love to each other and multiply themselves. They were afforded complete freedom as long as they remained in a dependent relationship with God. They could have lived forever in the presence of God, who provided for all their needs.

The Fall and Its Results

Satan, and a horde of fallen angels, were also present in the universe. The Lord had commanded Adam and Eve not to eat from the tree of the knowledge of good and evil or they would die (Genesis 2:17). Satan questioned and twisted God's command and tempted Eve through the same three channels of temptation that exist today, which were the same three channels that Satan used to tempt Jesus: "the lust of the flesh and the lust of the eyes and the boastful pride of life" (1 John 2:16 NASB). Deceived by the craftiness of Satan, Eve defied God and ate the forbidden fruit, and Adam chose to follow in her defiance and ate as well.

Adam and Eve died spiritually, meaning that their intimate relationship with God was severed. Their souls were no longer in union with Him. Later they died physically, which is also a consequence of sin (Romans 5:12). Their perfect life in the Garden was ruined by their choice to sin. Filled with guilt and shame, "the eyes of both of them were opened, and they realized they were naked; so they sewed fig leaves together and made coverings for themselves...and they hid from the LORD God among the trees of the garden" (Genesis 3:7,8).

The fall affected Adam and Eve's life in many ways. First, *it darkened their minds*. Trying to hide from God revealed they had lost a true understanding of who their Creator was, since no one can hide from an omnipresent God. They were darkened in their understanding because they were separated from the life of God (Ephesians 4:18). Even today the natural person cannot understand spiritual things, "because they are spiritually discerned" (1 Corinthians 2:14).

Second, *the fall affected their emotions*. The first emotion expressed by Adam after the fall was fear. When God confronted the pair, Adam said to Him, "I was *afraid* because I was naked; so I hid" (Genesis 3:10). To this day, anxiety disorders are the number-one mental health problem of the world, and "fear not" is the most repeated command in Scripture.

Those who live in guilt and shame want to hide and cover up. Fear drives them away from anything that would expose their inner world. Without God's unconditional love and acceptance, they run from the light or try to discredit its Source. Unable to live up to God's eternal standards of morality, they face the prospect of continuing to live in guilt and shame, or like Adam, they blame someone else (Genesis 3:12).

Third, *the fall also affected Adam and Eve's will*. Before they sinned, they could make only one wrong choice: to eat from the tree of the knowledge of good and evil, which was forbidden. Every other choice they could make in the Garden was a good choice. Once Adam and Eve made that one bad choice, they were confronted every day with many good *and* bad choices—just as we are today. Other than the presence of God in our lives, the responsibility to choose is the greatest power we possess. We can choose to pray or not pray, believe God or not believe Him. We can choose to yield or not yield to a variety of temptations presented to us. Sexual bondage is the result

---

A STEP OF MATURITY

The tendency of the Western church is to acknowledge the three channels of temptation but not acknowledge the role of Satan the tempter. Consequently, the problem is limited to the influences of this fallen world and the ongoing struggle with the flesh. This provides an inadequate answer for recovery. In the context previous to where the apostle John presents the three channels of temptation, he twice defines young men in the faith as those who "have overcome the evil one" (1 John 2:13,14). According to verse 12, "Little children" in the faith are forgiven. In other words, they have overcome the penalty of sin, whereas young men in the faith have overcome the *power* of sin.

of wrong choices, or never having the knowledge of what the right choices are.

The entire world is still choosing to eat from the tree of the knowledge of good and evil without the tree of life. The result is intellectual arrogance, pride, self-sufficiency, self-adulation, self-centeredness, self-gratification…self, self, and more self. Self-sufficiency is the greatest enemy to our sufficiency in Christ. Pride is what caused Lucifer to fall, and pride will keep many people from coming to the Light.

We Need the Light

As a result of the fall, we are spiritually dead, helpless, and without any hope of escaping the bondage of sin, outside of the life we can have in Christ. No person living independently of God can live a righteous life or withstand the conviction of His perfect light.

> Everyone who does evil hates the light, and will not come into the light for fear that his deeds will be exposed. But whoever lives by the truth comes into the light, so that it may be seen plainly that what he has done has been done through God (John 3:20-21).

The first step in recovery is to face the truth and acknowledge our sin. We need to come out of the darkness and face the truth in the light. That is the initial thrust of salvation. "He rescued us from the domain of darkness, and transferred us to the kingdom of His beloved Son" (Colossians 1:13 NASB). Many people have told me they want to get out of their addictive behavior because they are tired of living a lie; and sexual sins, abuse, and addictions are the easiest to lie about. The effects of food addictions (overeating, anorexia, or bulimia) are revealed by our physical appearance. Drug or alcohol addiction will affect our behavior and performance, which are noticeable to others.

Those living in sexual bondage, however, display clues less obvious to others, with the exception of doctors who treat sexually transmitted diseases. You can be the president of the United States and be sexually addicted, but if you are chemically addicted, I doubt you could be the president of anything for very long. Those who are addicted to chemicals are usually sexually addicted as well, but they seldom seek treatment for their sexual addiction unless they are exposed.

A Rebel Usurps Authority

When Adam and Eve sinned, Satan usurped their dominion over the earth and became the god of this world. When Jesus was tempted, Satan offered Him the kingdoms of the world if He would bow down and worship him (Luke 4:6). Jesus didn't dispute Satan's claim to earthly spiritual authority and even referred to him as "the prince of this world" (John 12:31; 14:30; 16:11). Paul called Satan "the prince of the power of the air" (Ephesians 2:2 NASB). As a result of Adam and Eve's fall, "the whole world is under the control of the evil one" (1 John 5:19).

The good news is that God's plan of redemption was under way immediately upon Satan's wresting authority from Adam and Eve. The Lord cursed the serpent and foretold the downfall of Satan (Genesis 3:14-15), which was accomplished by Christ on the cross. Ultimate authority in heaven and earth belong to Jesus. Satan's days of ruling over the kingdoms of this world are numbered.

Being physical descendants of Adam and Eve, we are all born spiritually dead and live under the dominion of Satan in the kingdom of darkness. But when we receive Christ, we are transferred from Satan's kingdom to God's kingdom (see also Philippians 3:20). Satan is still the ruler of this world, but he is no longer *our* ruler. Jesus Christ is the Lord of our lives. The deceiver can't do anything about our position in Christ—but if he can get us to believe that our identity and position in Christ aren't true, we will live as though they aren't.

Even as members of Christ's kingdom we are still vulnerable to Satan's accusations, temptations, and deceptions. If we give in to his schemes, Satan can influence our thinking and therefore our behavior. If we remain under his influence long enough and fail to resist him, Satan will gain a measure of control in our lives. Much of his dominance is sexual. However, even if we believe his lies, we will remain

God's children, because we have been bought and purchased by the blood of the Lamb, who will never leave us nor forsake us.

Paul warns us about this spiritual deception in 1 Timothy 4:1; "The Spirit clearly says that in later times some will abandon the faith and follow deceiving spirits and things taught by demons." Paying attention to deceiving spirits is what kept Rick, whose story I shared in the introduction, in bondage. Before he became a Christian, he made sinful choices that led to sexual bondage. He hadn't recovered from his sexual abuse, and he chose to be sexually promiscuous. After he gave his life to Christ, the father of lies tempted him to seek gratification of his fleshly desires. The more he tried to satisfy the flesh, the bigger it grew. Only after Rick understood his identity and position in Christ and exercised the spiritual authority that every believer has in Christ was he able to break free of his sexual bondage and the lies that accompany it.

The Seeds of Sexual Bondage

It has been my privilege to help thousands of people find their freedom in Christ. Nearly every one of them has had some kind of sexual problem. The ongoing cosmic battle between God's kingdom and the kingdom of darkness is often manifested in sexual sin, because sex is the means by which the seeds of reproduction are sown in either kingdom.

Christians who respect and obey God's directives in Scripture regarding sexual purity are sowing seeds in the kingdom of God that will reap a harvest of peace and righteousness. People who ignore God's call to sexual purity are sowing seeds in Satan's kingdom and will reap a harvest of pain and heartache. The fruit of the seeds sown in these two kingdoms greatly impacts our world and our family relationships. Adultery and incest destroy ministries and tear up families for generations. Secret sin on earth is open scandal in heaven.

One of Satan's primary weapons for ruining relationships is sexual impurity. More Christian marriages and ministries are destroyed through sexual misconduct than for any other reason. People who are living in secret sexual bondage have no joy in marriage or ministry, and cannot grow in their relationship with God. Conversely, believers who pursue a life of moral purity are bearing fruit in the kingdom of God. The result is a positive impact for righteousness on their marriages, children, friends, and co-workers.

The strong link between Satan's kingdom of darkness and sexual bondage was illustrated to me during one of my conferences. David was referred to us by the pastoral staff of the host church. He was a successful businessman who appeared to have everything going for him. However, his wife had just filed suit for divorce because of his addiction to pornography. One of our staff met with him to take him through the Steps to Freedom in Christ.

As we lead people through the Steps, we sometimes discern that they need to renounce any previous involvement in satanic or occult activities, even if they don't remember any. As David renounced making any covenants with Satan, he was shaken to the core when the Lord revealed to him an experience from his past. He recalled a nightmarish encounter in his room at night with a spiritual presence who offered him all the sex and girls he wanted if he would just tell it he loved it. At first David refused, not sure if he was awake or dreaming. Then he gave in and said he loved Satan. Sowing that seed in Satan's kingdom resulted in the sexual bondage that was ruining David's life and marriage. His recovery began when he renounced that decision, took his place in Christ, exercised the authority he has in Christ, and resisted the devil, who fled from him.

If the concept of a spiritual battle is new to you, consider Paul's words in 2 Corinthians 4:1-4:

> We have renounced the things hidden because of shame, not walking in craftiness or adulterating the word of God, but by the manifestation of truth commending ourselves to every man's conscience in the sight of God. And even if our gospel is veiled, it is veiled to those who are perishing, in whose case the god of this world [Satan] has blinded the minds of the unbelieving so that they might not see the light of the gospel of the glory of Christ, who is the image of God.

THE ABNORMAL BECOMES THE NORMAL

Mass sexual perversion precipitated the fall of Rome. How close is America coming to a similar demise? Pornography used to be hard to locate, but now every hotel room is a porno parlor—and so is every office at work or room in our homes that has a computer connected to the Internet. Canada and many states are moving rapidly to legalize homosexual "marriages." Movies and television programs are portraying homosexual individuals and couples as the "liberated" ones who must set straight the "unenlightened." Anybody standing for traditional sexual morality is considered a bigot or "homophobe."[1]

This is actually a carefully planned strategy, as explained by Pastor Kevin Shrum in an article written in the November 25, 2007, issue of the Nashville *Tennessean:*

In 1989, Marshall Kirk and Hunter Madsen published a book entitled *After the Ball: How America Will Conquer Its Fear and Hatred of Gays in the '90s.* They laid out a plan for normalizing behavior that had previously been viewed as deviant. First, desensitize the citizen to deviancy by making deviancy appear positive. Second, make people feel guilty about their perceived bigotries, often equating homosexual and race bigotry. Third, through the media, display as normal that which had previously been viewed as abnormal.

God's Design

Perversion of God's design for both reproduction and sexual relations is rampant wherever the kingdom of darkness flourishes. In the Old Testament, pagans honored Molech, a detestable Semitic deity, by the fiery sacrifice of their children—their seed—a practice God strictly prohibited (Leviticus 18:21; 20:1-5). There were many other pagan gods in biblical times whose worship involved sexual perversity. Chemosh, the national deity of the Moabites, required the sacrifice of children, and Diana of Ephesus had an explicitly sexual nature. Devotion to *anyone* or *anything* other than our Creator is idolatry, and idolatry always leads to some kind of immoral perversion.

However, the devil has never been able to do more than temporarily stop God's plan for propagating morally pure children of God and filling the earth with them. After the fall, God countered Satan's offensive by presenting a plan for redemption through the seed of the woman (Genesis 3:15). Satan was behind Pharaoh's order to kill all the male babies in Egypt when God was raising up Moses to deliver His people (Exodus 1–2).

When Christ was born, Herod issued a decree that all male babies under the age of two were to be killed. The Lord told Joseph about the plot in a dream, and he took Mary and the infant Jesus to Egypt (Matthew 2:7-23). Today, as we watch the heartless aborting of millions of unborn children in the name of "choice," we have to wonder what great deliverance God has in store for His people and ask, "What is Satan trying to hinder this time?"

Unable to prevent the birth of the Messiah, Satan prompted Judas, one of the Lord's own disciples, to betray Him. That devious plan played right into God's hand. The grave could not hold Jesus, and His resurrection sealed Satan's fate forever. Satan is a defeated foe. In spite of today's perversion of sex and reproduction, we have hope. God has a plan, and it will succeed.

The timetable of God's redemptive plan, however, is related to the church, as revealed by Paul in Ephesians 3:8-12:

> To me, the very least of all saints, this grace was given, to preach to the Gentiles the unfathomable riches of Christ, and to bring to light what is the administration [how God is working out His plan] of the mystery [something previously not revealed] which for ages has been hidden in God who created all things; so that the manifold wisdom of God might now be made known through the church to the rulers and authorities in the heavenly places [Satan's hierarchy]. This was in accordance with the eternal purpose which He carried out in Christ Jesus our Lord, in whom we have boldness and confident access through faith in Him.

During this present age, God is working out His plan through the church and is making His wisdom known through the church to the kingdom of darkness. Since that is the eternal purpose of God, there are several issues that we as the church need to consider.

First, *God is going to work through the church,* Christ's body. This is one reason why our ministry is church-based, and why I seek to provide resources to support the work of the local church.

Second, *we are in a spiritual battle,* and that is why we are instructed to put on the armor of God, stand firm, and take every thought captive to the obedience of Christ.

Third, *our ministry is reconciliation.* We must learn how to help God's children remove the barriers to their intimacy with their heavenly Father through genuine repentance and faith in Him. God's children cannot grow or bear fruit if they are living in bondage to sin.

Fourth, *we have to minister in love under the New Covenant of grace.* There is no condemnation for those who are in Christ Jesus (Romans 8:1). Nobody likes to live in bondage. Such people don't need a critic—they need a guide who can show them the way out of their bondage to sin. And that is what the rest of this book is about.

QUESTIONS FOR DISCUSSION AND THOUGHT

1. How would you contrast the "naked and unashamed" sexual experience of Adam and Eve with what we experience today?

2. How did the fall affect Adam and Eve mentally, emotionally, and volitionally (in their wills) and how does that relate to us today?

3. Why do we see the three channels of temptation but fail to see the tempter, or why does the Western church have the tendency to acknowledge our struggle with the world and the flesh but not the devil?

4. How can self-sufficiency keep us in bondage, and how does that relate to self-help efforts that are so common today? Does trying harder work?

5. Why do many people not seek the help they need?

6. What is Satan trying to accomplish by enticing us to sexual sins?

7. What is the strategy to desensitize North American culture to sexual sins? Is it working?

8. What is the "eternal purpose of God," and how can the church work with God to fulfill that purpose?

2

GOD HAS A PLAN

*When sex is divided from love there is a feeling that one
has been stopped at the vestibule of the castle of pleasure.*

FULTON SHEEN

As the story goes, a French teacher was explaining to her class that in French, unlike English, nouns are designated as either masculine or feminine. For instance, *house* is feminine—*la maison;* and *pencil* is masculine—*le crayon.*

A student asked, "What gender is *computer?*" Instead of giving an answer, the teacher split the class into two groups, men and women, and asked them to decide for themselves whether *computer* should be a masculine or a feminine noun. Each group was asked to give four reasons for their conclusion.

The men's group decided that *computer* should definitely be the feminine gender—that is, *la computer*—because

1. No one but their creator understands their internal logic;

2. The native language they use to communicate with other computers is incomprehensible to everyone else;

3. Even the smallest mistakes are stored in long-term memory for possible later review; and

4. As soon as you make a commitment to one, you find yourself spending half your salary on accessories for it.

The women's group, however, concluded that *computer* should be masculine—that is, *le computer*—because:

1. In order to do anything with them, you have to turn them on;

2. They have a lot of data, but still can't think for themselves;

3. They are supposed to help you solve problems, but half the time they *are* the problem; and

4. As soon as you commit to one, you realize that if you had waited a little longer, you could have gotten a better model.

⋄⇒⊚⇐⋄

God created us sexual beings—male and female. Our gender is determined at conception, and our entire sexual anatomy is present at birth. The molecular structure of a skin sample—even that of an infant—will reveal our sex, as will our saliva (female athletes are gender-tested by taking a sample of it from their mouths). Sexual identity is coded in our DNA. God is not anti-sex; He created sex! David proclaimed, "You created my inmost being; you knit me together in my mother's womb. I praise you because I am fearfully and wonderfully made; your works are wonderful" (Psalm 139:13-14).

Viewing sex as evil is not an appropriate response to what God created and pronounced good. "Everything God created is good, and nothing is to be rejected if it is received with thanksgiving, because it is consecrated by the word of God and prayer" (1 Timothy 4:4-5). On the other hand, Satan is evil, and sin distorts what God created. Denying our sexuality and fearing open discussion about our sexual development is playing into the devil's hand. We need to tell our congregations and our families the truth about our sexual nature and help them all live morally pure lives.

A Plan for the Ages

God's ideal plan for marriage was outlined in the Garden of Eden before Adam and Eve sinned: "A man will leave his father and mother and be united to his wife, and they will become one flesh" (Genesis

2:24). A monogamous and heterosexual marriage under God was His divine intention—one man and one woman forming an inseparable union and living in dependence upon Him.

Adam and Eve were also commanded by God to procreate and fill the earth with their offspring. Had they never sinned, perhaps the world today would be populated with a race of sinless people living in perfect harmony. Adam and Eve's sin in the Garden marred God's beautiful plan. Lest we be too hard on them, however, had any of us been in the Garden instead of them, we probably would have done the same thing. Adam and Eve enjoyed ideal conditions, lived in perfect light, and still sinned. It is unlikely that we would have done any better.

Despite the fall, God did not abandon His plan for the man and the woman and their sexual relationship. Rather, He selected the procreative process of human marriage as the vehicle for redeeming fallen humanity. God covenanted with Abraham, saying, "In your seed all the nations of the earth shall be blessed, because you have obeyed My voice" (Genesis 22:18 NASB). The "seed," or descendant, God was talking about was Christ (Galatians 3:16), who would bless the whole world by providing salvation through His death and resurrection.

There was another facet to God's plan for marriage in redemptive history. The covenant relationship of marriage between husband and wife is a God-ordained picture of the covenant relationship between God and His people. The church is called the bride of Christ (Revelation 19:7), and God desires to receive to Himself a bride who is holy and blameless, "without stain or wrinkle or any other blemish" (Ephesians 5:26-27). The purity and faithfulness of a Christian marriage is to be an object lesson of the purity and faithfulness God desires in our relationship with Him.

The Bible prohibits sexual immorality for two interrelated reasons. First, unfaithfulness or sexual sin violates God's plan for the sanctity of human marriage. When you become sexually involved with someone other than your spouse—whether physically, or mentally through lust and fantasy—you shatter God's design. You bond with that person, thus blemishing the "one man and one woman" image, and you break the covenant with your spouse (1 Corinthians 6:16-17). We were created to become one flesh with only one other person of the opposite sex. When you commit sexual sin with another, you become one flesh physically and mentally, resulting in sexual bondage. That's why Paul calls this a sin against your own body.

Second, when you commit adultery, you deface the image of God's covenant relationship with His people, which your marriage was designed to portray. Think about it: A loving, pure, committed relationship between a husband and wife is God's illustration to the world of the loving, pure, committed relationship He desires with His body, the church. Every act of sexual immorality among His people tarnishes that image.

The Plan in the Old Testament

Not many generations passed before the descendants of Abraham found themselves in bondage to Egypt. God raised up Moses to deliver His people and provide them a law to govern their relationships in the Promised Land, including their sexual relationships. Six of the ten commandments listed in Exodus 20 touched on marital fidelity.

1. *You shall have no other gods before me* (verse 3). Sexual sin violates this commandment because it elevates sexual pleasure above our relationship with God. God is a jealous God. He won't tolerate a rival, including the "god" of our impure appetites.

2. *Honor your father and your mother* (verse 12). Sin of any kind, including sexual sin, brings shame and dishonor to your parents.

3. *You shall not commit adultery* (verse 14). God ordained sex to be confined to marriage. Adultery—sex outside of marriage—is a sin against your marriage partner and God (Genesis 39:9).

4. *You shall not steal* (verse 15). Adulterers rob their spouses

of the intimacy of their relationship and steal sexual pleasure from their illicit partners.

5. *You shall not give false testimony* (verse 16). Marriage is a
covenant made before God and human witnesses. Sexual
sin breaks the marriage vow. In effect, the unfaithful
partner lies about being faithful to his or her spouse.
Adulterers often continue lying to cover up their sin.

6. *You shall not covet* (verse 17). To covet is to desire something that doesn't belong to you. All sexual sin begins
with a desire for someone that is not rightfully yours.

Though most are written in the negative, the commandments of
God are not restrictive—they are protective. God's intention was to
prevent a fallen humanity from sowing more seeds of destruction
through sexual immorality and thus enlarging the realm of the kingdom of darkness.

God's law also specified heterosexuality and condemned homosexuality. His people were to maintain a clear distinction between
a man and a woman even in appearance: "A woman must not wear
men's clothing, nor a man wear women's clothing, for the LORD your
God detests anyone who does this" (Deuteronomy 22:5).

Homosexual "marriages" and sexual relations were also clearly
forbidden: "Do not lie with a man as one lies with a woman; that is
detestable" (Leviticus 18:22); in 20:13, "If a man lies with a man as one
lies with a woman, both of them have done what is detestable. They
must be put to death; their blood will be on their own heads." (In the
2003 case of Gene Robinson, rather than stone such a person to death,
an apostate church made him a bishop! A gracious church would love
the man but hate the sin—and work to restore his fallen nature.)

God commanded Adam and Eve and their descendants to multiply
and fill the earth. The only way they could obey that command was to
procreate through the means of sexual intercourse as men and women.
Men can't have children by men, and women can't have children by

women. The debased lifestyle of homosexuality is in direct conflict with God's plan of populating the earth, and He detests it.

God also instructed His people regarding the spiritual purity of their marriages:

> You shall not intermarry with [pagan nations]; you shall not give your daughters to their sons, nor shall you take their daughters for your sons. For they will turn your sons away from following Me to serve other gods; then the anger of the LORD will be kindled against you, and He will quickly destroy you (Deuteronomy 7:3-4 NASB).

Ironically, the most glaring example of disobedience to this command is found in the man reputed to be the wisest who ever lived. King Solomon had 700 wives and 300 concubines, including some from the nations with whom God expressly prohibited intermarriage (1 Kings 11:1-2). "His wives turned his heart away after other gods; and his heart was not wholly devoted to the LORD his God" (11:4). We cannot have God-honoring marriages if we seek spouses who are not children of God.

When I studied in Israel, I saw a memorial of what happens to the kingdom of God when the king violates God's commandments. Outside the walled city of Jerusalem is a place called "the hill of shame." It was on this hill that King Solomon allowed his foreign wives to build temples to other gods. Israel divided into two nations after the death of Solomon and never returned to the prominence it once enjoyed. The hill is still barren and stands as a silent reminder of the fruit of disobedience.

The Old Testament also assures us that God designed sex within the confines of marriage for pleasure as well as procreation. The Song of Solomon portrays the joys of physical love in courtship and marriage. Furthermore, the law directed that the first year of marriage should be reserved for marital adjustment and enjoyment: "When a man takes a new wife, he shall not go out with the army nor be charged with any duty; he shall be free at home one year and shall give happiness to his wife whom he has taken" (Deuteronomy 24:5 NASB).

Satan's Assault

Satan's assault on God's design of heterosexuality is evident in the account of Sodom and Gomorrah. When angels appearing as men visited Lot in Sodom, all the men of the city, young and old, clamored to have them brought outside for a homosexual orgy. God cut off this evil seed-line by destroying the two cities (Genesis 19:1-29). Even today we use the term *sodomy* to describe unnatural acts of sexual intercourse, such as oral and anal sex between males.

Israel continued to battle idolatry—and the sexual immorality that always attends it—throughout Old Testament history. When Israel split into two kingdoms, Israel and Judah, both nations degenerated spiritually and morally, despite the commandments of the law and the warnings of the prophets. Both nations were judged for their sins. God raised up Assyria to destroy Israel, and Judah was conquered by Babylon and taken into exile.

The Old Testament ends on a sad note. Only a remnant of God's people returned from captivity to the land God had given them. For most of the following 400 years the stronger neighbor nations pushed them around like puppets. On the eve of Christ's birth, the Jews were in political bondage to Rome and in spiritual bondage to their apostate leaders. The glory of God had departed from Israel. It must have appeared to many that Satan had completely foiled God's plan.

But God still had a plan. Even though the moral and spiritual fabric of Israel had been shredded, He miraculously preserved the seed of Abraham: the Redeemer who would sit upon the throne of David. Abraham's seed—Jesus Christ—was about to make His entrance (John 1:14). The blessing of Abraham was soon to be extended to all the nations of the world in Christ.

God's Plan Under the New Covenant

God's plan for Christian marriages after the cross—in a world still saturated by the darkness of sin—is given in 1 Thessalonians 4:3-5:

This is the will of God, your sanctification; that is, that you

abstain from sexual immorality; that each of you know how
to possess his own vessel in sanctification and honor, not
in lustful passion, like the Gentiles who do not know God
(NASB).

The word "possess" means to acquire or take for yourself. The word
"vessel" is translated "wife" in 1 Peter 3:7. Thus verse four could read,
"That each of you know how to take a wife for himself in sanctification and honor." God's design for marriage is the same in the New
Testament as it was in the Old Testament: monogamous, heterosexual
marriages under Him that are free of sexual immorality.

Any sexual activity outside God's design is forbidden because it
is counterproductive to the process of sanctification. In other words,
don't expect to reap the fruit of the Spirit and enjoy fulfillment as a
Christian if you are sowing seeds in Satan's kingdom through sexual
immorality. Knowing that God's will for our lives is our sanctification
(1 Thessalonians 4:3) is the basis for the following six specific instructions relating to sex.

YOU CAN'T SERVE TWO MASTERS

My first attempt at discipling a young college man failed miserably. No
matter how I tried to help him, he couldn't seem to get his spiritual life
together. I was baffled. During that time, he was dating one of the nicest
young Christian women in the college group. Finally we stopped our
futile attempt at discipleship.

Two years later he confessed that, while I had been trying to disciple him, he had been sleeping with several coeds, though not with
the woman he had been dating. He admitted he had written me off after
he had heard me talk about sexual purity. He wanted to be a growing
Christian, but he wasn't about to give up his sexual lifestyle. There is little
wonder why my attempt to disciple him hadn't been working.

---

1. We Are to Abstain from Premarital Sex

It has become common, even expected, in our culture for couples to sleep together and even live together before marriage or in lieu of marriage. They justify their actions by saying, "Love is what counts—who needs a marriage certificate?" or "How can we know if we're sexually compatible unless we sleep together?" The world places a high value on physical attraction and sexual compatibility in finding a partner. Christians are far from immune to this influence. During my early years of ministry, 18 of the first 20 Christian couples I counseled before marriage admitted to me they had slept together—and that was many years ago, from 1972 to 1974.

Fornication is not God's way to seek a life partner. Outward appearance and sexual appeal may attract a person to a potential mate, but neither has the power to hold a couple together. Physical attraction is like perfume or cologne. You smell the fragrance when you put it on, but within minutes your sense of smell is saturated and you barely notice the scent. Similarly, unless you go beyond physical attraction to know and love the real person, the relationship won't last…because there really is no relationship. Sex becomes a selfish animal act instead of an intimate means of expressing love between a male and a female child of God.

Christian dating is not like shopping for a good-looking, comfortable pair of shoes. Shoes get scuffed, worn, and dated, and you have to replace them every year or two. Christian dating is the process of finding God's will for a lifetime marriage partner. Commitment to Christ and godly character far outweigh physical attraction and sex appeal when it comes to marriage.

2. We Are to Abstain from Extramarital Sex

Doug and Katy came to see me because they were having marital problems. In an angry moment, Doug had told his wife she didn't satisfy him sexually like a previous girlfriend had. In tears, Katy told me how hard she tried to be like that other girl, which was impossible for her. The couple left my office without resolution.

Shortly thereafter, Doug came home and saw Katy sitting on the couch with a pillow on her lap. She asked him if he loved her. He said he did. Katy replied, "Then I'm going to make you pay for what you said about me for the rest of your life!" She pulled his handgun from under the pillow and shot herself to death.

I am aware this is an extreme illustration, but multiple partners cannot help but lead to comparisons. Almost every wife fears that her husband will be unfaithful and can sense when another woman is looking at her man. Then she will compare herself to that other woman.

It is normal to be attracted to a mate by his or her appearance, personality, and other qualities. Christian marriage, however, is a commitment to stay faithful "'til death do us part." Once you are married, all comparisons must end. You will likely be introduced to someone who looks better than your spouse, who seems more sensitive and caring, and may even be more spiritual, but it doesn't matter. Your commitment is to your spouse and no one else. The best-possible-mate contest is over, and you and your spouse have both won!

As Christians, our first commitment is to Christ, which is the most important relationship we have. Your marriage is a picture of that union, and no other relationship must be allowed to deface that image. The pathway to marital happiness and fulfillment is found in loving and serving your spouse, not in looking for someone you think may bring you greater happiness or sexual pleasure.

Many people who end up in extramarital affairs say they are bored with their spouses sexually. They're not bored with their partners, actually—they're bored with sex because they have depersonalized it. When the focus is on self-centered sex and the partner is viewed as a sex object, boredom is likely. When the focus is on nurturing the total relationship and fulfilling the dreams and expectations of your mate, marital life—including sex—remains a fulfilling experience.

When we make a commitment to get married, we should also make a commitment not to entertain contrary thoughts. Rest assured you will be tempted to. Throughout your married life you will look at someone else and wonder what it would be like to be married to him or her. From that point on, everything in your mind is pure fantasy.

You don't have a clue what it would be like to be married to someone you don't really know.

Consider the boss who has an excellent secretary, one who looks after his every need in unquestioning obedience. He starts to think she would make an excellent spouse. So he divorces his wife and marries his secretary. The morning after the wedding he wakes up and asks his new wife to make him a cup of coffee. She says, "Make it yourself—I'm not your secretary anymore!"

3. We Are Not to Violate the Conscience of Our Spouse

A number of years ago I conducted a one-day conference entitled "For Women Only." The participants were invited to ask me questions on any topic. Embarrassing questions were written out and dropped in a basket. Most of the written questions were about sex, and most of those centered on the question, "Must I submit to anything my husband wants me to do sexually?"

If the question is, "Should I submit to anything my husband *needs* sexually?" the answer is yes. According to 1 Corinthians 7:3-5, husbands and wives are not to withhold their bodies from each other:

> The husband should fulfill his marital duty to his wife, and likewise the wife to her husband. The wife's body does not belong to her alone but also to her husband. In the same way, the husband's body does not belong to him alone but also to his wife. Do not deprive each other except by mutual consent and for a time, so that you may devote yourselves to prayer. Then come together again so that Satan will not tempt you because of your lack of self-control.

You are not to withhold sex from your spouse or use it as a weapon against him or her. Doing so gives Satan an opportunity to tempt both of you in areas where you lack self-control.

But should a wife submit to anything her husband *wants* her to do sexually? No. Neither spouse has the right to violate the conscience of the other. If a sexual act is morally wrong for one, it is morally wrong for both. One man protested, "But Scripture says that the wedding bed is undefiled." I told him to read the whole verse: "Marriage should be honored by all, and the marriage bed kept pure, *for God will judge the adulterer and all the sexually immoral*" (Hebrews 13:4).

Demanding that your spouse violate his or her conscience to satisfy your lust violates the wedding vow of loving one another and destroys the intimacy of a relationship built on trust. A person can and should meet the legitimate sexual needs of his or her marriage partner. In no way, though, should you demand that your spouse try to satisfy your lust. First, your spouse can't. Only Christ can resolve your problem with lust. The more you feed lustful desires, the more they grow. Second, it is degrading and demeaning to demand that your spouse perform sexual acts against his or her conscience. Only Christ can break that cycle of bondage and give you the freedom to love your spouse as Christ loved the church.

4. We Are to Abstain from Sexual Fantasy

The tempting thought to pull off the freeway and rent a sexually explicit video was overwhelming. Scott was married, with two children still living at home, but he struggled with sexual fantasies. As he sped closer to the off-ramp, a conflict raged within him. He knew his actions wouldn't be pleasing to God. He knew he would feel ashamed when it was all over. He knew he would be humiliated if his wife or children came home unexpectedly and found him acting out his fantasy. But he was propelled to the video store like a heroin addict to a fix.

Scott had found many ways to satisfy his secret craving for sexual excitement and release: pornographic paperback novels and magazines, textbooks on the subject of sexuality, sexual fantasies while in the shower, and steamy videos featuring nudity and sex (he avoided the more obvious X-rated films, reasoning that the R-rated ones were easier to explain if he got caught).

He ignored the "way of escape" provided to him by God and took the familiar exit off the freeway. He made his selection in the video shop and headed home for an afternoon of sexual fantasy. After watching the sexually graphic movie, he was overwhelmed with shame and guilt. *How did I get sucked into this pattern again?* he agonized. *Lord, what am I going to do?* He had told no one about his struggle and repeated failures—not his wife, not his pastor, not even the two Christian counselors he had seen in the past for related problems. He felt weak, helpless, and alone. Even God seemed distant and unavailable. So Scott just stuffed his feelings and continued his charade of being the model Christian.

Sexual fantasy plagues many Christian men and women. They may not be physically involved in premarital or extramarital sex, but they have numerous affairs in their minds—an endless variety of sexual adventures with people they know, characters in books, magazines, or video screens, and phantom lovers they dream up on their own. Most sexual fantasy addicts find release in masturbation, which can escalate into extramarital affairs.

Sexual fantasy may be regarded by many as harmless self-pleasuring, but Christians are to seek mental purity for at least three different reasons.

First, according to Jesus' words in Matthew 5:27-29, *the seeds for adultery are sown in the heart:*

> You have heard that it was said, "Do not commit adultery." But I tell you that anyone who looks at a woman lustfully has already committed adultery with her in his heart. If your right eye causes you to sin, gouge it out and throw it away. It is better for you to lose one part of your body than for your whole body to be thrown into hell.

Jesus says we should cut off our right hand as well *if* it is necessary—but it isn't necessary, and that is not where the problem lies. If that were the answer, we would all be cutting off body parts and become bloody torsos rolling down the aisles of our churches...and we still wouldn't have solved the problem.

The passage teaches that looking is the evidence that adultery has already been conceived in the heart. In the same chapter, in verses

21 and 22, Jesus teaches that anyone who is angry with his brother is guilty before the court, and that calling one's brother a name is the same as murder. That would make us all guilty of adultery and murder! In a very real sense, we are! In the Sermon on the Mount, Jesus is teaching what constitutes genuine righteousness. It is not merely external conformity to the law, which we can't do anyway. He is teaching that the seeds of murder and adultery are sown in our hearts and minds.

To solve the problem, something has to be done about our heart—and God *has* done something. Ezekiel prophesied that God would give us a new heart and a new spirit (11:19-20; 18:31; 36:26). The heart is the center of our self. Only in the heart do the mind, emotions, and will converge. We can intellectually acknowledge the truth, but if it doesn't touch our hearts, it will not change our character. When the truth does penetrate our hearts, our emotions and our will are affected. "Above all else, guard your heart, for it is the wellspring of life" (Proverbs 4:23). To have victory over sin, we have to win the battle for our mind and keep our heart pure.

Second, according to James 1:14-15, *sexual immorality in the mind precipitates a sexually immoral act:* "Each one is tempted when, by his own evil desire, he is dragged away and enticed. Then, after desire has conceived, it gives birth to sin; and sin, when it is full-grown, gives birth to death." We may think our sexual fantasies will never be acted out, but eventually "out of the overflow of the heart the mouth speaks" (Matthew 12:34). What is sown and nurtured as a seed in the heart will eventually flower as a deed.

Third, *sexual fantasy depersonalizes sex and devalues people.* Sexual fantasy is not a shared marital relationship but a breeding ground for lust and self-gratification that mushrooms out of control. When sex becomes boring (which it certainly will with the mentality of "all take and no give"), a person will likely look for a more exciting partner.

One man assured me that his sexual fantasizing was not a sin because he visualized girls without heads! I told him, "That's precisely the problem. You have depersonalized sex." This is what pornography does. Sex objects are never properly valued as people created in God's image, much less someone's daughter or son. Treating someone as an object for personal gratification goes against everything the Bible teaches about the dignity and value of human life.

5. We Are to Abstain from Out-of-Control Masturbation

Masturbation is seen by some as a harmless, pleasurable means of releasing sexual pressure. Those who practice, condone, or recommend it say it is a private way of gratifying sexual needs without fear of disease or pregnancy.

The Bible is virtually silent on the topic of masturbation, and Christians have widely divided opinions about it. Some believe it is a God-given means to release pent-up sexual energy when we are unmarried or when our mate is unavailable. In that sense, they believe masturbation can be a means of sexual self-control. At the other extreme are Christians who condemn it as a sin.

Those in favor remind us that it is nowhere condemned in the Bible, that it poses no health risks, and that it may help prevent acts of sexual immorality. Those opposed state that it is sex without a marriage partner and therefore wrong, because it is self-centered, that it is accompanied by sexual fantasies, and that it can lead to an uncontrollable habit.

I certainly don't want to add any restrictions that God doesn't teach, nor do I want to contribute to legalistic condemnation that is already being heaped on people. But why do so many Christians feel guilty after masturbating? Is it because the church or their parents have said it is wrong, and therefore the guilt is only psychological? If so, the condemnation springs from a conscience that has been developed improperly. The condemnation may also come from the accuser of the brethren (Revelation 12:10), who plagues every sexual addict.

To consider if masturbation is contributing to your sexual bondage, ask yourself the following questions:

1. Are you committing the mental adultery that Jesus condemned?

2. Are you seeking to put pornographic images in your mind?

3. Has masturbation replaced sexual intimacy in your marriage?

4. Can you stop masturbating? (If you can't, then you have lost some degree of self-control.)

5. Do you sense the Holy Spirit's conviction when you masturbate?

Perhaps you are able to masturbate without depriving your spouse or defiling your mind. Hopefully, you are not chained to the act and can stop at will. If you can't, there is encouraging hope for you if you are trapped in the web of sexual fantasy and out-of-control masturbation. God has provided a way of escape for every temptation.

As you struggle to gain your freedom in Christ, remember that "there is now no condemnation for those who are in Christ Jesus" (Romans 8:1). Guilt and shame do not produce good mental health—but love, acceptance, and affirmation do. God loves you, and He will not give up on you. You may despair in confessing again and again, but His love and forgiveness are unending.

6. We Are to Abstain from Homosexual Behavior

God's view of homosexuality hasn't changed, even though it is politically correct to accept this "alternate lifestyle." The New Testament places homosexuality in the same category as other sexual sins to be avoided:

> Do not be deceived: Neither the sexually immoral nor idolaters nor adulterers nor male prostitutes nor homosexual offenders nor thieves nor the greedy nor drunkards nor slanderers nor swindlers will inherit the kingdom of God (1 Corinthians 6:9-10).

Some people argue, "But I was born this way. I have always had homosexual tendencies. I can't help it—this is the way God created me." God did not create anyone to be a homosexual. He created us male and female. Homosexuality is a lie. There is no such thing as a homosexual; there are homosexual *feelings, tendencies,* and *behaviors.* Neither did God create pedophiles, adulterers, or alcoholics. If a person can rationalize homosexual behavior, why can't another rationalize adultery, fornication, pedophilia, and so on?

Because of the fall, we are all genetically predisposed to certain strengths and weaknesses. Some people can become addicted to alcohol faster than others, but that does not make them alcoholics. They become chemically addicted because they *choose* to drink—in order to party without inhibitions, or cope with life, or stop the pain. Some boys may have lower levels of testosterone and develop more slowly than others, or are raised by overbearing, abusive parents, or are sexually exploited, but that does not make them homosexuals. Coming to terms with our past and the lies we have believed is crucial for our recovery in Christ.

A university professor attended a conference I was conducting. He was a married man with children who from the time of his youth had feared the possibility that he was gay. He told me later that hearing the above truth set him free. He was believing a lie. Two years later I was doing the same conference in a neighboring city and he came to help us counsel others. In those two years he had led 62 men out of sexual bondage to freedom in Christ.

⋯⊷⊶⋯

For some sad reason, our culture is bent on finding the ultimate sexual experience without regard for whether it is right or wrong, oblivious to the inevitable consequences. When we think we've found it, we sadly discover that the pleasures last for only a season, so the quest must continue. You cannot satisfy the lusts of the flesh. Growing Christians are bent on pursuing the ultimate personal relationship:

"Blessed are those who hunger and thirst for righteousness, for they shall be satisfied" (Matthew 5:6 NASB). Are you willing to pursue the greatest of all relationships, the one that every child of God can have with his heavenly Father? If so, you will be satisfied.

EXODUS FROM THE TRAP OF HOMOSEXUALITY

My personal stand on this issue is certainly not politically correct, nor does it represent the position of the scientific establishment. The official Web site for the American Psychological Association states, "The reality is that homosexuality is not an illness. It does not require treatment and is not changeable." It goes on to warn that conversion therapy is poorly documented and could cause potential harm. The American Psychiatric Association's Web site adds, "There is no published scientific evidence supporting the efficacy of 'reparative therapy' as a treatment to change one's sexual orientation."[2]

There is now! Christian psychologists Stanton Jones and Mark Yarhouse have conducted research in conjunction with the organization Exodus International over several years. They tested the impact of ex-gay programs on participants—whether they actually experienced change, and whether the attempt to change caused additional stress. Their findings as of this writing have contradicted the established professional consensus, which they report in their book *Ex-Gays?: A Continuing Study of Religiously Mediated Sexual Orientation Change in Exodus Participants*.

There has not been any formal research on the effectiveness of the message and method of Freedom in Christ Ministries in helping people get out of sexual bondage, but we welcome it. (We have had formal research conducted on several other psychological issues, which I will share later.) The truth is, we are having tremendous success helping God's children get out of sexual bondage, including homosexual lifestyles. This is not because there is anything special about us. Rather, our method, as explained in *Discipleship Counseling* (Regal Books, 2003), is based on the presence of the Living God who came to set captives free.

If you long to be right with God and desire to be free in Christ, you can be!

QUESTIONS FOR DISCUSSION AND THOUGHT

1. This chapter shows the standard God has set for sexual conduct and orientation. How does that make you feel?

2. Why is it important to know that the covenant relationship of a Christian marriage is a picture of the covenant relationship the church has with Christ? How does sexual sin distort that image?

3. Do the Ten Commandments address the issue of sexual morality? How?

4. Sanctification is God's will for our lives. How does that relate to marriage and sexual purity?

5. Why are we to abstain from premarital sex?

6. Why are we to abstain from extramarital sex?

7. Why should we not violate the conscience of our spouse?

8. What is wrong with sexual fantasy?

9. Is masturbation wrong, and if so, why?

10. Why do you think society is so out of step with the Bible's standard concerning homosexuality?

3

REAPING THE HARVEST

*Continence is the only guarantee of an undefiled
spirit, and the best protection against the promiscuity
that cheapens and finally kills the power to love.*

GENE TUNNEY was speaking to a group of high-school students about sex. A "not yet" Christian young man was there with his Christian girlfriend. After a series of questions he asked, "If I had sex with my girlfriend before we got married, would I later regret it?" That was a great question from a wise young man. "Yes," I said, "there are consequences to every decision we make."

What goes up must come down. If you jump off a tall building without the benefit of a parachute, hang glider, or bungee cord, you will drop to the sidewalk like a rock. Plant watermelon seeds and you will harvest watermelons if you nurture the plant. Everything we do and every choice we make has consequences. Cause and effect is built into the universe, and we will reap what we sow.

If we sow seeds of sexual purity, we will reap the benefits in marriage. If we sow seeds of sexual immorality, we will reap a dark harvest of negative personal and spiritual consequences. "The one who sows to his own flesh will from the flesh reap corruption, but the one who sows to the Spirit will from the Spirit reap eternal life" (Galatians 6:8 NASB).

What are the consequences of sowing to the flesh in reference to sexual conduct? What kind of corruption is Paul talking about? First, there are the obvious outward or physical and relational consequences, which we will deal with in this chapter. Second, there are the inward or spiritual consequences, which we will explore in the next chapter.

The Harvest Experienced in Body and in Marriage

The most obvious consequences of ignoring God's design for sex and marriage are the physical and relational consequences. Physical pain, the threat of disease and death, and the breakup of a relationship are quickly noticed and felt. So-called "free" sex isn't free, and those who pursue it aren't living in freedom.

Sexual promiscuity leads to disgusting forms of bondage. And the potential price tag in terms of health alone is staggering. Sexually transmitted diseases (STDs) "add billions of dollars to the nation's healthcare costs each year" and "are difficult to track. Many people with these infections do not have symptoms and remain undiagnosed...These 'hidden' epidemics are magnified with each new infection that goes unrecognized and untreated."[3]

Medical health experts insist that STDs are by far the most prevalent of communicable diseases. The problem is no longer epidemic, but pandemic.

The most frightening aspect of STDs is that they can be passed on without the carrier exhibiting any symptoms. This is especially true for those who test positive for HIV. Victims may go for years without showing signs of illness, unknowingly passing on the disease to their sexual partners, who in turn pass it on to other unsuspecting victims. Without medical testing, people cannot be sure their sexual partners are free of all sexual diseases. Indeed, partners may not even know they are infected. The rapid spread of STDs in our culture illustrates the chilling truth that a sexual encounter involves more than two people. If you have sex with a promiscuous person, as far as STDs are concerned, you are also having sex with every one of that person's previous sex partners, and you are vulnerable to the diseases carried by all of them.

People who have violated God's design for sex also pay a price in their marriage relationships. Women who have had unholy sex don't seem to enjoy holy sex. I have counseled many women who, because of past sexual experiences, can't stand to be touched by their husbands. Incredibly, their feelings change almost immediately after finding their freedom in Christ. One pastor had been refused sexually by his wife for ten years because of bondage that had blocked her from sexual intimacy. To their mutual surprise, the couple was able to come together after she had resolved her personal and spiritual conflicts.

Promiscuity before marriage leads to lack of sexual fulfillment in marriage. The euphoria that comes from sex outside God's will quickly dissipates and leaves the participant in sexual bondage. If the past sexual sins were consensual, the bondages only increase as the individual attempts to satisfy his or her lust, which can't be satisfied. The more lustful habits are fed, the faster they grow. If the sins were not consensual, meaning that the person participated in the act but didn't want to or was forced to, then he or she will not be able to enjoy wholesome marital relations until the past is resolved. Such people lack the freedom to enjoy mutual expressions of love and trust.

If people have been victims of severe sexual abuse, such as rape or incest, their bodies have been used unwillingly as instruments of unrighteousness. (The biblical basis for this statement will be shared later.) Tragically, these victims have become one flesh with their abusers and have great difficulty relating to their spouses in a healthy way. It's not fair that these people were violated against their will. It's sick, and the sickness pollutes what should be a fulfilling and intimate marriage relationship. The good news is that people can be set free from the bondage caused by such violations. They can renounce the unrighteous uses of their body, submit to God, resist the devil, and forgive those who abused them.

The Defilement of a Family

One of the most heartrending consequences of sexual sin is the effect it has on the children of the offender. The affair between King David of Israel and Bathsheba, wife of Uriah the Hittite, illustrates the downward spiral of personal defilement and its effect on the family. Even though David is called a man after God's own heart (Acts 13:22), he had a dark blot on his life. The words of 1 Kings 15:5 summarize his life: "David had done what was right in the eyes of the LORD and had not failed to keep any of the LORD's commands all the days of his life—except in the case of Uriah the Hittite." Because of his moral failure, David's family paid a steep price. Let's consider his steps to defilement and their tragic consequences.

"One evening David got up from his bed and walked around on the roof of the palace. From the roof he saw a woman bathing. The woman was very beautiful, and David sent someone to find out about her" (2 Samuel 11:2-3). There was nothing wrong with Bathsheba being beautiful, and there was nothing wrong with David being attracted to her.

That's the way God made us. Bathsheba may have been wrong for bathing where others could see her, and David was definitely wrong for continuing to look at her. For such occasions, God provides a way of escape. David could have turned and walked away from the tempting sight, but he didn't.

When David sent messengers to get Bathsheba, he was far down the path of defilement—making the possibility of stopping more difficult with each step. The two slept together, and she became pregnant. David tried to cover up his sin by calling Uriah, Bathsheba's husband, home from the battlefield, with the expectation that he would sleep with her. The pregnancy could then have been attributed to Uriah, but this noble man wouldn't cooperate. He didn't want to have any privileges his men didn't have. So David sent him back to the battlefield and arranged for him to be given an assignment in which he would likely be killed. Now David the adulterer was David the murderer!

Sin has a way of compounding itself. If you think living righteously is hard, try living unrighteously. Cover-up, denial, and guilt make for a very complex life.

After a period of mourning the death of her husband, Bathsheba became David's wife. David actually suffered physical consequences because of his guilt and shame. In Psalm 32:3 he describes his torment: "When I kept silent, my bones wasted away through my groaning all day long. For day and night your hand was heavy upon me; my strength was sapped as in the heat of summer."

The Lord allowed David plenty of time to acknowledge his sin. The king didn't confess, so God sent the prophet Nathan to confront him. God won't let His children live in darkness for long, because He knows it will eat them alive. One pastor with a pornography addiction traveled to a pastors' conference. His colleagues asked for copies of his ministry materials, and when he opened his briefcase with a crowd around him, he suddenly realized that he had brought the wrong case. His stack of smutty magazines was there for all to see! Was it embarrassing? Of course! But was it tragic? No! The exposure caused this man to finally seek the help he needed. "There is nothing concealed that will not be disclosed, or hidden that will not be made known" (Matthew 10:26).

Sadly, the public lives of many Christians are considerably different from their private lives. As long as they think the facade can continue, they will likely not deal with their own issues. Ironically, these people are often the ones who are most critical of others. People who haven't dealt with their own guilt and shame often seek to "balance their internal scales" by projecting guilt and blame on others. The Lord says in Matthew 7:1-5,

> Do not judge, or you too will be judged. For in the same way you judge others, you will be judged, and with the measure you use, it will be measured to you.
>
> Why do you look at the speck of sawdust in your brother's eye and pay no attention to the plank in your own eye? How can you say to your brother, "Let me take the speck out of your eye," when all the time there is a plank in your own eye? You hypocrite, first take the plank out of your own eye, and then you will see clearly to remove the speck from your brother's eye.

Forgiveness and Consequences

David finally acknowledged his sins, both of which were capital offenses under the law. Then Nathan declared, "The LORD has taken away your sin. You are not going to die. But because by doing this you have made the enemies of the LORD show utter contempt, the son born to you will die" (2 Samuel 12:13-14).

The enemies of the Lord are Satan and his angels. I don't think the average sinning Christian has a clue concerning the moral outrage his or her sexual sins cause in the spiritual realm. Satan, the accuser of the brethren, throws them into God's face day and night (Revelation 12:10). Our private, secret sins are committed openly before the god of this world and his fallen angelic horde! Far worse, our sexual sins are an offense to God, who is grieved by our failure and who must endure the utter contempt of Satan. In addition, our hypocrisy is known by the world and our witness is compromised.

The Lord spared David, but his and Bathsheba's son died. Why did he have to die? It is possible that God had to cut off the rebellious seed sown by David so that the male offspring of this adulterous relationship did not receive the birthright! We are talking about the throne of David, upon which the Messiah would reign. God took the infant home to be with Himself, and David had the assurance that he would be with the child in eternity (2 Samuel 12:23).

Additional judgment was meted out to David's household as a result of his sin. The prophet Nathan further declared,

> This is what the LORD says: "Out of your own household I am going to bring calamity upon you. Before your very eyes I will take your wives and give them to one who is close to you, and he will lie with your wives in broad daylight. You did it in secret, but I will do this thing in broad daylight before Israel" (2 Samuel 12:11).

The Lord's word was fulfilled when Absalom, one of David's sons, "lay with his father's concubines in the sight of all Israel" (2 Samuel 16:22).

Amnon, another son of David, followed his father's example to an even more despicable level of sexual immorality (2 Samuel 13). His lust for his virgin half sister Tamar, Absalom's sister, provoked him to play on her sympathies with a feigned illness. When Tamar came to his room to take care of him, Amnon tried to seduce her. When she refused his advances, he raped her. Apparently Amnon could have gone through legitimate channels to take Tamar as his wife. But his lust demanded to be satisfied *now*.

Great calamity came upon David as a result of his sin. In all, four of his sons died prematurely: Bathsheba's son died at birth, Amnon was killed by his brother Absalom in retaliation for the rape of Tamar, and Absalom and Adonijah were both killed attempting to take the throne from their father. All this came upon David because he failed to turn away from the tempting sight of a woman bathing.

Nature or Nurture...or Is It Spiritual?

In the Ten Commandments, God said,

> You shall not make for yourself an idol, or any likeness of what is in heaven above or on the earth beneath or in the water under the earth. You shall not worship them or serve them; for I, the LORD your God, am a jealous God, visiting the iniquity of the fathers on the children, on the third and the fourth generations of those who hate Me, but showing lovingkindness to thousands, to those who love Me and keep My commandments (Exodus 20:4-6 NASB).*

God blesses those who are obedient to His covenant to the thousandth generation, but the iniquities of those who are disobedient are passed on to the third and fourth generations.

How does this happen? Anybody working with hurting people knows that the abusers have been abused themselves. The cycle of abuse is a well-attested social phenomenon. Do we inherit a specific bent toward sin from our parents—and if we do, is this transmission

---

* See also Deuteronomy 5:9-10; Exodus 34:6-7; Deuteronomy 7:9-10; and Numbers 14:18.

genetic (nature), environmental (nurture), or spiritual? I believe the correct answers are *yes* and *all three!* First, there is plenty of evidence to show we are genetically predisposed to certain strengths and weaknesses. However, we cannot blame genetics for our own bad choices.

Second, environmental factors definitely contribute to sinful behavior being passed on from one generation to the next. For example, if you were raised in a home where pornography was readily available and sexual promiscuity was modeled, you would certainly be influenced in this direction. Unless parents deal with their sins, they unwittingly set up the next generation to repeat their moral failures. Jesus said, "A student is not above his teacher, but everyone who is fully trained will be like his teacher" (Luke 6:40).

Third, there seems to be an inherited spiritual bent toward sin as well. For instance, Abraham lied about his wife, calling her his sister. Later his son Isaac did exactly the same thing. Then Isaac's son Jacob lied in order to steal his brother's birthright, and told many other lies as well. This is a spiritual phenomenon. Nobody is suggesting that Abraham said to Isaac, "Listen, son, if you ever get in a jam, just pass your wife off as your sister. It didn't work for me, but maybe it will for you."

How It Happens

In the Old Testament, the Israelites confessed both their sins and iniquities and also those of their ancestors. Iniquities relate more to a rebellious spirit or strong will. Somehow these iniquities are passed on from one generation to another. Old Testament scholar S.J. De Vries explains this:

> In its early development Israel was very much influenced by a dynamic concept of corporate sin...The family group was a much more significant entity than the individual person. When the head of such a group transgressed, he transmitted guilt to every member of it...Thus, according to the Decalogue [Ten Commandments]...the iniquity of the father is to be visited upon the children.[4]

THE LEGACY OF IDOLATRY

Concerning idolatry, the prophet Hosea mentions demonic spirits affecting children, which is related to the parents' sins:

> They consult a wooden idol and are answered by a stick of wood. A spirit of prostitution leads them astray; they are unfaithful to their God. They sacrifice on the mountaintops and burn offerings on the hills, under oak, poplar and terebinth, where the shade is pleasant. Therefore your daughters turn to prostitution and your daughters-in-law to adultery (Hosea 4:12-13).

The cause of the children's sexual sins is not only the parents' sin of Idolatry, but also the demonic "spirit of prostitution."

How did the Israelites deal with ancestral sins? Here are some examples:

> Those of Israelite descent had separated themselves from all foreigners. They stood in their places and confessed their sins and the wickedness of their fathers (Nehemiah 9:2).

> I confess the sins we Israelites, including myself and my father's house, have committed against you (Nehemiah 1:6).

> O LORD, we acknowledge our wickedness and the guilt of our fathers; we have indeed sinned against you (Jeremiah 14:20).

> We have not obeyed the LORD our God or kept the laws he gave us through his servants the prophets. All Israel transgressed your law and turned away, refusing to obey you.
> Therefore the curses and sworn judgments written in the Law of Moses, the servant of God, have been poured out on us, because we have sinned against you (Daniel 9:10-11).

God had spoken, and the prophets had warned the people about generational sins. However, in the early sixth century BC, the prophet Ezekiel had to correct an abuse:

> The word of the LORD came to me: "What do you people
> mean by quoting this proverb about the land of Israel: 'The
> fathers eat sour grapes, and the children's teeth are set on
> edge?' As surely as I live, declares the Sovereign LORD, you
> will no longer quote this proverb in Israel" (Ezekiel 18:1-3).

This popular Israelite proverb was not from the book of Proverbs, nor was it from the mouth of God. The problem Ezekiel was trying to correct was a fatalistic response to the law and the abdication of personal responsibility. Children are not guilty because of their parents' sins and they will not be punished for their parents' iniquities, which are visited upon them, if they are diligent to turn away from the sins of their parents:

> [Ezekiel] did not mean to deny corporate sin: this was
> beyond dispute. [His] purpose was to accentuate individual
> responsibility, which was in danger of becoming submerged
> in a consciousness of overpowering national calamity. Even
> though the nation was now suffering a bitter corporate pun-
> ishment, there was hope for the individual if he would repent
> [see also Jeremiah 31:29-30].[5]

Sowing Seeds of Repentance

We have seen in the Old Testament the transmission of sin from one generation to the next, and how the prophets called the people to confess their sins and the sins of their fathers. An unholy inheritance cannot be dealt with passively. We must consciously take our place in Christ and renounce the sins of our ancestors. We are not guilty of our parents' sins, but because they sinned, their sins may be passed on to us. That is why we are told in Leviticus 26:40 to confess our own sin and the sin of our forefathers "in their unfaithfulness which they committed against Me, and also in their acting with hostility against Me" (NASB). The opposite is to cover up and defend the sins of our parents, grandparents, and others, and continue in the cycle of bondage.

The possibility of overcoming generational sins is evidenced in the life of Joseph, one of Jacob's sons. Joseph chose not to follow in the ways of his father, grandfather, and great-grandfather, even though he was given every opportunity to lie to protect himself from his jealous brothers. In fact, the more he told the truth, the more trouble he endured. If he was predisposed to lying, he chose not to comply. Eventually he was totally vindicated for his honesty.

I frequently minister to people who repeat the sins of their parents and grandparents. Are they forced to do these things? No! But they will repeat them if they continue to hold iniquity in their hearts, which can be visited to the third and fourth generations.

Under the Old Covenant, as we saw, all of God's chosen people were called to repent of their sins and iniquities regardless of whether the scope of their offenses was personal or national. National or corporate repentance cannot happen without individual repentance. This is not just an Old Testament concept. Paul wrote, "Just as sin entered the world through one man, and death through sin, and in this way death came to all men, because all have sinned..." (Romans 5:12). Peter wrote that we have been redeemed from our "futile way of life inherited from [our] forefathers" (1 Peter 1:18 NASB).

No matter what our ancestors have done, if we repent and believe in Christ, God rescues us from the dominion of darkness and brings us into the kingdom of His dear Son (Colossians 1:13). We are under a New Covenant, which promises, "Their sins and lawless acts I will remember no more" (Hebrews 10:17).

Repentance Breaks the Chain

Repentance is God's answer to sin and iniquity. Truth sets us free, but we won't experience that freedom without repentance. Repentance literally means "a change of mind," but it isn't genuine unless we have turned away from our sins and iniquities and turned toward God and the truth. Members of the early church began their public profession of faith by literally facing the west and declaring, "I renounce you, Satan, and all your works and ways." Then they would face the east and proclaim their faith in God. In so doing, they reclaimed any ground they or their forefathers had given to Satan. You will be given an opportunity to do this in the final chapter.

It is important to understand that God has forgiven us even before we repent, but He doesn't necessarily take away the natural consequences of our sin. If He did, it wouldn't take us long to figure out that we could sin all we want and then turn to God for cleansing without any repercussions. If you have contracted an STD, in all likelihood you will still have it after you have fully repented.

It is also important to realize that when parents repent, there is no guarantee their children will. Even if they were predisposed genetically, environmentally, and spiritually in the direction of your sin, your children are still responsible for their own choices. They may choose to repeat or not to repeat your failures, as well as your successes. Have you ever noticed that bad health is contagious, but good health isn't? Paul wrote, "Do not be misled: 'Bad company corrupts good character'" (1 Corinthians 15:33). Your children may have "caught" your bad habits from you, but they won't necessarily catch repentance from you. However, your repentant, healthy, God-fearing lifestyle will hopefully influence them to make their own choice to renounce sin and trust Christ.

An Example to Follow

David's sexual sin and cover-up by murder was tragic, and the consequences of sin in his own life and in the lives of his children were painful and long-lasting. However, David's own personal story has a good ending. He responded to his sin correctly and went on to shepherd Israel with integrity of heart and lead them with skillful hands (Psalm 78:72). His seed-line provided the human link for the Satan-crushing soul-Redeemer promised in Genesis 3:15.

David's confession of sin in Psalm 51 is a model prayer for those who violate God's plan for sexual purity:

Have mercy on me, O God, according to your unfailing

love; according to your great compassion blot out my transgressions. Wash away all my iniquity and cleanse me from my sin.

For I know my transgressions, and my sin is always before me. Against you, you only, have I sinned and done what is evil in your sight, so that you are proved right when you speak and justified when you judge…

Create in me a pure heart, O God, and renew a steadfast spirit within me. Do not cast me from your presence or take your Holy Spirit from me. Restore to me the joy of your salvation and grant me a willing spirit, to sustain me (verses 1-4,10-12).

There is one major difference, however. David related to God under the Old Covenant. We have the privilege of relating to God under the New Covenant. Under the grace of God, we are forgiven, and He will *never* leave us or forsake us. He has also given us a new heart and a new spirit. With God's love and presence in our lives, we can win this battle because the war has already been won.

So don't be discouraged with the sobering reality of the natural consequences of sinful choices. God loves you, because God is love. It is His nature to love you, and that is why His love is unconditional. Life without Christ is a hopeless end, but life with Christ is an endless hope. Be encouraged—Jesus Christ has broken the power of sin, defeated the devil, given you a new life in Himself, and set you free. You may not feel free right now, but keep reading, and don't stop until you have worked through the last chapter.

QUESTIONS FOR DISCUSSION AND THOUGHT

1. Why do you think the general public is not aware of the STD epidemic?

2. Why don't some people consider the consequences of their actions when being tempted?

3. Is private consensual sex really private? That is, are those engaging in it the only ones affected by their decision?

4. Is there such a thing as "secret sin"?

5. Can you think of a modern example of one person's sin having a negative effect upon others, like that of David?

6. How are the sins and iniquities passed on from one generation to the next?

7. Do you think it is necessary to confess your sins and the sins of your ancestors? Why or why not?

8. Are we ever guilty of our parents' sins?

9. What is repentance, and how is it different from confession?

4

THE
ADDICTION
CYCLE

*Some psychological and sociological conditioning occurs
in every person's life and this affects the decisions they
make. But we must resist the modern concept that all sin
can be explained merely on the basis of conditioning.*

FRANCIS SCHAEFFER

Dear Neil:

I was raised in what everyone would think was the perfect
home. My parents were Christians and were very involved
in the church. Not just involved, they were pillars. They were
not abusive, mean, or critical. In fact they went out of their
way to demonstrate their love and service to the Lord by
caring for children other than their own.

When I reached puberty, I was interested in sex, just like
every other red-blooded boy. My father and mother were
not very good at sharing on the intimate level, so most of
what I learned was from a book they had in the house. From
that book I learned how to masturbate. Pretty soon I was a
slave to masturbation. I soon found pornography, and was
enslaved to it also. It was available at any store, and they
didn't care whether a junior-high-school student bought it.
I was in my own private little world. On the outside I was
this Christian kid, involved with youth group, a counselor
at Christian camp, and a member of the "perfect family" at

church. On the inside I was in complete bondage to pornography and lustful thinking. Magazines, adult bookstores, peep shows, movie theaters—you name it, I saw it.

I went to a good Christian college, where I continued to feed my lustful habits. I knew where the stores were that sold pornography, and just like you mentioned in one of your books, I would justify my going there.

I married my beautiful Christian girlfriend, and to everyone around us we were the "perfect couple." But I still had this private world my wife didn't even know about. Now it was easier because I was on the road with my job. Things continued to get worse and I got closer and closer to the edge (adultery). I always thought I could dabble in pornography and never commit the "big one." Well, of course it finally happened, and then it happened again, and then again. All the while I knew it was wrong, I knew I shouldn't be doing what I was doing, but I couldn't stop. I would have guilt and remorse, but never true repentance.

Finally, events that I know were orchestrated by God led to my wife finding out about what I had done, and I finally confessed to her and to God my life of bondage to pornography and sex. I fell to my knees before God and repented of my sin, and for the first time truly felt the love and grace of my heavenly Father.

With the help of your books *Victory over the Darkness* and *The Bondage Breaker* I was able to discover my freedom in Christ. Never before have I felt such freedom! I am truly alive in Christ. No more bondage! No longer a slave to sin!

My wife has struggled through this with me, and we have received some additional help for our marriage. Praise God that we are doing better than we ever have, and Christ is finally in the center of our home and the center of my life. Thank you for your ministry and your work to help people like me to find their freedom.

I have received many letters like the one above. I share it with you to illustrate some key points. First, you can have the best parents in the world and still fall into sin. It is wrong to vilify parents, because it is their children who make the wrong choices. Yes, parents can pass on their sins and iniquities, but when children stumble that cannot always be assumed. Second, you can carry on a charade for a season, but your private life will eventually be exposed if you are a true believer. God will see to it, because He doesn't want any of His children to live in bondage. Finally, there is hope and freedom for those who really want it.

We have no indication that King David's parents set him up for sin, but we do know that he set up his children for sin, and God did expose what he did. I'm sure he deeply regretted his sinful choice to have sex with Bathsheba. Now let's look further into the story of his son Amnon and see how he deteriorated into raping his half sister Tamar. As with David, it began with an innocent infatuation and progressed to mental obsession: "Amnon son of David fell in love with Tamar...Amnon became frustrated to the point of illness on account of his sister Tamar, for she was a virgin, and it seemed impossible for him to do anything to her" (2 Samuel 13:1-2).

What Amnon called love was really lust, as evidenced by his selfish behavior. Solomon warned in Proverbs 6:25-26, "Do not lust in your heart after her beauty or let her captivate you with her eyes, for the prostitute reduces you to a loaf of bread, and the adulteress preys upon your very life." Tamar was not a prostitute, but the sexual fantasy in Amnon's mind had been replayed so many times that he was physically sick. He had looked lustfully once too often. The opportunity to find the way of escape was gone. The affair in his mind had been played over many times. Lust fueled by sexual fantasy screams for expression. So Amnon and his friend Jonadab concocted a plan to get Tamar into Amnon's bed.

Once a plan to fulfill the demands of lust is set in motion, it is seldom stopped. Amnon had lost control, and where there is no self-control, reason is gone. Amnon's lust had reduced him to a "loaf of bread." He was "like one of the wicked fools in Israel" (2 Samuel 13:13).

Ironically, right after his violation of Tamar, "Amnon hated her with intense hatred. In fact, he hated her more than he had loved her. "Amnon said to her, 'Get up and get out!'" (2 Samuel 13:15). Amnon didn't love Tamar. He never once considered what was best for her. He was trapped in a cycle of sexual addiction. People living in bondage hate that which controls them. Alcoholics crave a drink, but when they have had their fill, they smash the bottle against the wall in remorse, only to buy another bottle when the craving returns. The pornography addict burns his magazines, tosses his X-rated videos into the garbage, and tells his lover he never wants to see her again. But when the fires of lust rekindle—as they always do—he's back to his old haunts, looking for a sexual fix. The downward spiral of sexual degradation is predictable.

The Addiction Cycle

The addiction cycle is basically the same for every form of bondage. The cycle begins with a baseline experience. It represents who we are and what we are experiencing at the time of our first exposure to sex, drugs, or alcohol.

There is an emotional–physical rush when we are stimulated by some sexual thought or experience—ending in a euphoric high, which quickly declines. Consider Max, a teenaged boy who notices a new girl in class. Jill is a real beauty in his eyes, and he feels a rush of emotion just looking at her. When Jill returns his glance with a smile, Max's face flushes and his heart races with excitement. He's never felt so good. When the bell rings and Jill walks out of class, Max returns to his baseline experience. The rush is over for now...but he liked what he felt. He can't wait to see Jill again and experience the rush.

For weeks Max steals little glances at Jill and feels his heart throb. Max is a normal boy and a Christian who has standards of sexual purity. He initially has Jill's best interest at heart. The attraction he has for her wins out over his fear of rejection, and he invites her out for a date.

Riding in the car with Jill brings the rush to new heights. When

THE ADDICTION CYCLE

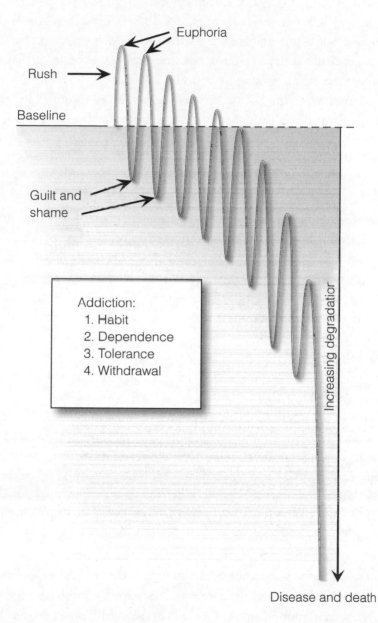

she innocently reaches over and touches his leg, Max almost flies out the window! They hold hands and end the date with a light hug. Max is in love. So far, so good. He has not compromised his standards, but he begins to imagine what it might feel like if they went a little further. Before long a hug and then a kiss from Jill don't give Max the same rush they did at first. To have the same euphoric experience, Max has to become a little more adventurous.

However, going further means he has to compromise his moral convictions just a little. Max has become more free with his hands during passionate good-night kisses. When he's alone he begins to fantasize about touching and kissing other parts of Jill's body.

The first step over the line brought him immediate gratification, and it was pleasurable. But as the euphoria declines, Max's conscience kicks in with twinges of guilt and shame. The flesh, however, wants to go further. Every new compromise brings greater conviction, which is followed by greater compromise. He discovers that a drink or a fix helps him overcome his inhibitions and dulls his conscience. Max—and perhaps Jill as well—is on a spiraling downward addictive cycle. He can stop, but does he want to?

Result: Bondage

The euphoric experiences of sexual and chemical highs wear off, and more stimulation is needed to get that same high. Every successive use or experience increases our tolerance to sex and chemicals. Alcohol and drugs may be used to overcome inhibitions. As lust grows, more stimulation is required to quench it. But it can't be satisfied. The more a fleshly desire is fed, the larger it grows. Normal sexual experiences don't seem to bring the euphoria that a simple touch once did. So other sexual experiences must be tried to get that same high. We want to have the first initial rush that felt so good, but greater levels of degradation take us further away, and our lifestyle has also moved far away from our baseline experience. Self-gratification dominates our thinking, and we have long since stopped considering the other person more important than ourselves (see Philippians 2:1-5). When we violate another person's conscience or moral boundaries, we have quenched the Spirit.

As the decline continues, a sexual habit brings an increasing dependence on the experience. The euphoria becomes a means of releasing stress and tension. The mind is filled with pornographic images and the memory of actual experiences. Many people in sexual bondage begin to withdraw from others and from God as the degradation continues. The unchecked cycle of sexual addiction opens the door to sexually transmitted diseases and even death for some. Those addicts with a strong conscience against violating others turn to self-gratification and pornography. Uncontrolled masturbation dominates their private world.

In a godly Christian marriage, love and trust are the means for having sexual intimacy, which can be extremely pleasurable for a husband and wife who love each other. For those who are sexually addicted, though, fear and danger replace love and trust. A married man shared that he filled his craving for "exciting" sex by carrying on an adulterous affair in a motel. He and his "lover" liked to perform sex with the curtains open or late at night in the motel swimming pool. For this man, sex with his Christian wife had become unexciting because his lust was reinforced by fear and danger.

Spiritual Degeneration Brings Physical Degradation

The shameful decline of sexual addiction is depicted in Romans 1:24-28:

> God gave them over in the sinful desires of their hearts to sexual impurity for the degrading of their bodies with one another. They exchanged the truth of God for a lie, and worshiped and served the created things rather than the Creator—who is forever praised. Amen.
>
> Because of this, God gave them over to shameful lusts. Even their women exchanged natural relations for unnatural ones. In the same way the men also abandoned natural relations with women and were inflamed with lust for one another.

Men committed indecent acts with other men, and received
in themselves the due penalty for their perversion.

Furthermore, since they did not think it worthwhile to retain
the knowledge of God, he gave them over to a depraved
mind, to do what ought not to be done.

Notice the progression: from shameful lusts to homosexuality to
a depraved mind. As a nation, America is probably between stages
two and three. There was a time when every state in the nation had
laws against sodomy. Now homosexuality is accepted as an alternative lifestyle and is protected by our courts. Our minds are becoming
increasingly depraved. The frightening thing is, a depraved mind is
devoid of logic. It can no longer reason morally. We are sliding completely off our moral foundation as a nation.

If you personally find yourself in this downward spiral, realize that
your degradation began when you exchanged the truth of God for a
lie and began worshiping created things rather than the Creator. In a
moment of temptation, you chose to follow lustful desires instead of
God's plan for moral purity. With every repeated negative choice, the
lie became more deeply entrenched. Satan, the "father of lies" (John
8:44), is winning the battle for your mind.

There are many ways in which we are tempted to exchange the
natural for the unnatural in the area of sexual behavior. One is the fascination with oral and anal sex. Before the so-called sexual revolution
of the 1960s, those acts were considered to be sodomy. Even today the
media uses the term *sodomy* when referring to oral sex. Young people
are experimenting with oral sex because they consider it "safe"—that
is, they can't get pregnant. But it's not safe or healthy when sexually
transmitted diseases are rampant. To show how far we have come
since even the 1960s, in 2003 the United States Supreme Court struck
down a Texas law against sodomy and essentially said no state can
regulate sexual standards for consenting adults. Today, teenagers don't
consider oral sex as "having sex." Whatever they may think, they are

still uniting themselves with each other outside of marriage, and this kind of union brings bondage.

Are oral and anal sex natural? Is that how God designed those body parts to be used? Was one person created to walk on his hands and another on his feet? From the standpoint of hygiene, is it natural to put the mouth so close to orifices designed for the elimination of bodily wastes? This aspect of the sexual revolution has helped homosexuality to proliferate, because you don't need the opposite sex to perform oral sex. Have we exchanged the truth of God for a lie?

Ignorance of the truth is no excuse. Paul clearly warned us that "the wrath of God is revealed from heaven against all ungodliness and unrighteousness of men who suppress the truth in unrighteousness, because that which is known about God is evident within them; for God made it evident" (Romans 1:18-20 NASB). Every conscious choice against the truth numbs the soul's awareness of it. Behaviors once seen as unnatural and indecent are passionately accepted as normal. The conscience becomes seared, and the awareness of God is dimmed.

God gives those who don't honor Him over to degrading passions. When the church at Corinth condoned an incident of sexual perversion, Paul instructed them, "Hand this man over to Satan, so that the flesh may be destroyed and his spirit saved on the day of the Lord" (1 Corinthians 5:5).

Throughout this degenerative process, God graciously offers a way back through Christ. No matter where people may be in their flight from light into darkness, there is safe passage home. The serial rapists and murderers on death row can throw themselves on the mercy of God and receive His forgiveness just like the thief on the cross. In God's economy, sin is not measured by quality or quantity. Jesus died once for *all* our sins.

Is there hope for those who haven't gone too far? Can we repent of our sinful ways and return to God? Of course we can, and freedom from sexual bondage is possible for every child of God who is willing to submit to God and resist the devil. We can have victory over sin if we understand and appropriate our position in Christ.

Mental Strongholds

When you first came to Christ, hopefully you learned you were a new creation "in Christ," and that old things had passed away. Not only that, you were transferred out of the kingdom of darkness into the kingdom of God's dear Son, and you are no longer "in Adam"—you are alive "in Christ."

All that being true, you have probably wondered why you still struggle with some of the same old thoughts and habits. Or maybe you came to Christ hoping that your sexual or chemical addiction would be resolved, but you still have the same cravings and thoughts. There is a logical and biblical explanation as to why that is so.

Because of the fall we were all born physically alive but spiritually dead (Ephesians 2:1). We had neither the presence of God in our lives nor the knowledge of His ways. So during those early and formative years, we all learned how to live our lives independently of God. Then one day we came to Christ, and everything I wrote two paragraphs back became true of us—but nobody pushed the "clear" button in our mind. Everything that had previously been programmed into our memories was still there. That is why Paul wrote, "Do not conform any longer to the pattern of this world, but be transformed by the renewing of your mind. Then you will be able to test and approve what God's will is—his good, pleasing and perfect will" (Romans 12:2).

Without Christ, we learned how to cope or defend ourselves as a means of survival. Psychologists call these survival techniques *defense mechanisms:* denial, rationalization, projection, blaming, lying, emotional insulation, and so on. They are also known as *flesh patterns* or *mental strongholds.* These mental habit patterns of thought are pathways grooved into our brains. It is similar to when a truck is driven along the same route in a pasture, rain or shine, every day for months. Deep ruts are formed, and it isn't long before the truck will just stay in the ruts without being steered. In fact, any attempt to steer out of the ruts is met with resistance.

Mental strongholds are assimilated into our mind from the environment in which we are raised in two ways. First, they are primarily developed in our mind through *prevailing experiences,* such as the homes we were raised in, the schools we attended, the churches we went to (or didn't go to), and the friends and enemies we encountered. Mental attitudes are more caught than formally taught. For example, neighborhood friends could have shown you pornographic magazines or experimented with you sexually. Babysitters could have fondled you sexually. Such experiences will have lasting effects on you unless they are dealt with.

The second major contributor to the development of strongholds in our mind is *traumatic experiences.* Whereas prevailing experiences are assimilated by our mind over time, traumatic experiences are burned into our memory because of their intensity—for example, the death of a parent, a divorce, incest, or rape. These experiences are stored in our memory bank and influence our thinking. We are not so much in bondage to these experiences as we are in bondage to the lies we choose to believe about God, ourselves, and life in general because of those traumas.

WE ARE STILL INDIVIDUALS WITH CHOICES

Assimilation from the environment isn't the only determinant of mental strongholds, because we each have individual choice. Two children can be raised in the same home by the same parents, eat the same food, play with the same friends, and attend the same church—yet respond differently to life events. We are individually created expressions of God's workmanship (Psalm 139:13-14; Ephesians 2:10). Despite similarities in genes and upbringing, our unique personalities and our capacity to make personal choices result in different evaluations of and responses to life.

As we struggle to reprogram our minds from the negative input of past experiences, we are also confronted daily with an ungodly world system. It is important to realize that we can continue to be conformed to this world, even as Christians, by believing lies, reading wrong material, and so on. There is no immunity from the enticements of this world; we can allow them to affect our thinking and behavior. "See to it that no one takes you captive through hollow and deceptive philosophy, which depends on human tradition and the basic principles of this world rather than on Christ" (Colossians 2:8).

Strongholds and Temptation

Since we live in this world, we will continuously face the temptation to conform to it. It is not a sin to be tempted, however. If it were, Christ would be the worst sinner who ever lived because He was "tempted in every way, just as we are" (Hebrews 4:15). Rather, we sin when we consciously choose to give in to temptation, which Christ never did.

All temptation is an attempt by Satan to get us to live our lives independently of God, to walk according to the flesh rather than according to the Spirit (see Galatians 5:16-23). Satan knows exactly which buttons to push when tempting us because he's a great observer of humanity. He knows your weaknesses and your family history. He's aware of the prevailing experiences and traumatic experiences that have made you vulnerable to certain temptations. Based on your past behavior, he knows your vulnerability to sexual temptations.

Each temptation begins with a seed thought in our mind stimulated by the world, the flesh, and the devil himself.

Some Typical Flesh Patterns

If we continue to act on wrong choices in response to temptation, a habit can be formed in about six weeks. If the habit persists, a stronghold will be developed in the mind.

We are constantly bombarded with sexually stimulating thoughts since sex is used in the media for "entertainment" and to sell everything from beer to bonds. Of course, pornography and illicit sexual activities reinforce and strengthen sexual strongholds, but many people don't even need the external world to fantasize, because they have programmed so much junk into their minds through the Internet, television, movies, books, and magazines. That's why sexual strongholds are difficult to overcome. Once images are formulated in the mind, the mental pictures are there for instant recall. An alcoholic can't get drunk by fantasizing about a bottle. A drug addict can't get high by imagining himself snorting cocaine. But sexaholics can carry on affairs in their minds and act them out in the privacy of their homes.

An inferiority complex is a major stronghold that many Christians struggle with. We aren't born with an inferiority complex. It comes from living in a competitive world where we compare ourself with someone who runs faster, thinks smarter, or looks prettier. If you are plagued by feelings of inferiority, chances are you were raised in a competitive atmosphere or you chose to compare yourself with others. No matter how hard you tried, you couldn't please your parents or teachers, and someone always outdid you. Your efforts were never quite good enough.

As a redeemed child of God, you now understand that you are inferior to no other person. But deeply ingrained thoughts and feelings from the past seem to drown out the love and affirmation you get from God and godly people. You feel trapped on a dead-end street, constantly searching for the acceptance that eluded you as a child. That's a stronghold—and it can only be torn down in Christ.

Consider the variety of strongholds that come from being raised in a home where the father is addicted to alcohol. He comes home drunk and abusive every night. His oldest son is strong enough to stand up to him. There is no way he's going to take anything from this drunk. The middle son doesn't think he can stand up to Dad, so he accommodates him. The youngest son is terrorized. When Dad comes home, he heads for the closet or hides under the bed.

Twenty years later, the father is gone and these three boys are now adults. When they are confronted with a hostile situation, how do you think they respond? The oldest one fights, the middle one accommodates, and the youngest one runs and hides.

A Sexual Stronghold

Homosexuality is a stronghold. Condemning those who struggle with this behavior, however, will prove counterproductive. They don't need any more condemnation. They suffer from an incredible identity crisis already. Overbearing authoritarianism is what has driven many to this lifestyle in the first place.

Most of those who struggle with homosexual tendencies or behaviors have had poor developmental upbringing. Sexual abuse, dysfunctional families (often where the roles of mother and father are reversed), exposure to homosexual literature before they had an opportunity to fully develop their own sexual identity, playground teasing, and poor relationships with the opposite sex have all contributed to their mental and emotional development. Mixed messages lead to mixed emotions.

Henry, a 62-year-old pastor, admitted to me that he had struggled with homosexual tendencies for as long as he could remember. More than once he had given in to those urges. He had begged God to forgive him and take the feelings away. He had attended healing services and self-help groups for those with sexual bondages. Nothing had worked. To his credit, Henry had never once given up on God. He was married and had somehow kept his struggle a secret from his children. (Most people in sexual bondage struggle privately. It is an extremely lonely battle.)

I asked Henry what his earliest childhood memory was. He went back to the age of two. His birth father had left before he was born, and his Christian mother raised him. She had a boyfriend, who occasionally came over and spent the night. On those nights, Henry had to share a bed with this man. His earliest childhood memory was of this man, whom he admired so much, turning his back to him and going to sleep. The little boy was desperately looking for affirmation from a male figure—wanting so much to be loved, accepted, and appreciated.

As I led him through the Steps to Freedom in Christ, Henry broke down and cried. He forgave his birth father for abandoning him, and he forgave the man who had slept in his bed for rejecting him. Then he renounced every sexual use of his body as an instrument of unrighteousness and gave himself and his body to the Lord. I also encouraged him to renounce the lie that he was a homosexual and declare the truth that God had created him to be a man.

No, I didn't cast a demon of homosexuality out of him. I don't believe there is a demon of homosexuality or a demon of lust flying around inflicting such maladies on hapless victims. Christians are deceived, tempted, and accused—Satan is the instigator and he takes advantage of their victimization. Simplistic thinking has hurt the credibility of the church. I have seen Christianity mocked on prime-time television by a parade of homosexuals and lesbians who have left the church because well-meaning Christians have tried to cast demons of homosexuality out of them.

Don't get me wrong—there is no question that Satan is a player in our problems, and his hierarchy of demons will tempt, accuse, deceive, and take advantage of any ground that is given to them. But we must have a more wholistic answer if we are going to see any lasting fruit.

⟡⟴⟳⟡

So far we have looked at God's design for sex and marriage. We have seen how Satan attempts to pervert God's design and direct our attention away from the Creator to self-centered desires of the flesh. We have considered the contributing factors to sexual bondage and listed the steps that lead to a dark dead end. Hopefully, we are now ready to turn our attention to God's answer.

Questions for Discussion and Thought

1. What is wrong about jumping to conclusions about people's sexual struggles and prematurely establishing blame?

2. When does innocent infatuation become sexual obsession?

3. Can you explain the addiction cycle?

4. What is *tolerance?*

5. How do you think America measures up according to the progressive degeneration mentioned by Paul in Romans 1:24-26?

6. Do you see any national evidence of a depraved mind?

7. What potential dangers does oral sex offer?

8. Why do Christians who are new creations in Christ still struggle with a lot of the same old thoughts and habits?

9. How are mental strongholds formed?

10. What is the connection between thoughts, feelings, and behavior?

5

THE ONE-STEP PROGRAM

The triumphant Christian does not fight for victory; he celebrates a victory already won.

REGINALD WALLIS

If God's Word so clearly commands people not to live in sexual bondage, why don't we just obey God and stop doing what He forbids? Because telling people that what they are doing is wrong does not give them the power to stop doing it. Paul declared, "If a law had been given that could impart life, then righteousness would certainly have come by the law. But the Scripture declares that the whole world is a prisoner of sin" (Galatians 3:21-22).

Even more revealing is Paul's statement that "the sinful passions aroused by the law were at work in our bodies" (Romans 7:5). The law actually has the capacity to stimulate what it prohibits. Forbidden fruit always appears more desirable. If you don't believe it, tell your child he can go *here* but he can't go *there*. The moment you say that, where does he want to go? *There!* Laying down the law does not remove sinful passions. The core problem is the basic nature of people—not their behavior, which just reveals who they are and what they have chosen to believe.

The Pharisees were the most law-promoting people of Jesus' day, but they were far from righteous. Jesus told His disciples, "Unless your righteousness surpasses that of the Pharisees and the teachers of the law, you will certainly not enter the kingdom of heaven"

(Matthew 5:20). Trying to live a righteous life externally when we are not righteous internally will only result in us becoming "whitewashed tombs, which look beautiful on the outside but on the inside are full of dead men's bones and everything unclean" (Matthew 23:27). The focus must be on what is inside, "for from within, out of men's hearts, come evil thoughts, sexual immorality, theft, murder, adultery, greed, malice, deceit, lewdness, envy, slander, arrogance, and folly. All these evils come from inside and make a man 'unclean'" (Mark 7:20-23).

The Secret of Victory: Our Identity in Christ

If trying harder to break the bonds of lustful thoughts and behavior and to live in sexual purity doesn't work, what will? Two verses in the Bible summarize what must happen in order for us to live righteously in Christ. First, "The reason the Son of God appeared was to destroy the devil's work. No one who is born of God will continue to sin, because God's seed remains in him" (1 John 3:8-9). If we are going to be set free from sexual bondage and walk in that freedom, our basic nature must be changed, and we must have a means for overcoming the evil one.

For those of us who are alive in Christ, these conditions have already been met, as the second verse tells us. God has made us partakers of His divine nature (2 Peter 1:4) and has provided the means by which we can live in victory over sin and Satan. What exactly happened to us?

Before we came to Christ, the following words described us:

> You were dead in your trespasses and sins, in which you formerly walked according to the course of this world, according to the prince of the power of the air [Satan], of the spirit that is now working in the sons of disobedience. Among them we too all formerly lived in the lusts of our flesh, indulging the desires of the flesh and of the mind, and were by nature children of wrath (Ephesians 2:1-3 NASB).

Before Christ, we were spiritually dead and under the domain of Satan.

But a change took place at salvation. Paul wrote, "You were once darkness, but now you are light in the Lord" (Ephesians 5:8). Our old nature in Adam was darkness; our new nature in Christ is light. We have been transformed at the core of our being. We are no longer "in the flesh"; we are "in Christ." Paul wrote, "Those who are in the flesh cannot please God. However, you are not in the flesh but in the Spirit, if indeed the Spirit of God dwells in you" (Romans 8:8-9 NASB).

Furthermore, before we became Christians we were under the dominion of the god of this world, Satan. But the moment we were saved, God "rescued us from the dominion of darkness and brought us into the kingdom of the Son he loves, in whom we have redemption, the forgiveness of sins" (Colossians 1:13-14). We no longer have to serve Satan or sin. We "have been given fullness in Christ, who is the head over every power and authority" (Colossians 2:10). We are free to obey God and walk in righteousness and purity.

All Our Needs Are Met in Christ

Paul says, "My God will meet all your needs according to his glorious riches in Christ Jesus" (Philippians 4:19). The most critical needs are the "being" needs, like eternal life. Jesus came that we might have life (John 10:10)—spiritual or eternal life. To be spiritually alive means that our souls are in union with God. In the Bible, that truth is most often communicated by use of the prepositional phrase "in Christ" or "in Him." And we have a new identity: "To all who received him, to those who believed in his name, he gave the right to become children of God" (John 1:12). "How great is the love the Father has lavished on us, that we should be called children of God! And that is what we are!" (1 John 3:1).

Our foundational "being" needs of acceptance, security, and significance are all met in Christ:

In Christ

I am accepted:

John 1:12   I am God's child

John 15:15   I am Jesus' chosen friend

Romans 5:1   I have been made holy and am accepted by God (justified)

1 Corinthians 6:17   I am united with the Lord and am one with Him in spirit

1 Corinthians 6:20   I have been bought with a price—I belong to God

1 Corinthians 12:27   I am a member of Christ's body— part of His family

Ephesians 1:1   I am a saint, a holy one

Ephesians 1:5   I have been adopted as God's child

Ephesians 2:18   I have direct access to God through the Holy Spirit

Colossians 1:14   I have been bought back (redeemed) and forgiven of all my sins

Colossians 2:10   I am complete in Christ

I am secure:

Romans 8:1-2   I am free from condemnation

Romans 8:28   I am assured that all things work together for good

Romans 8:31-34   I am free from any condemning charges against me

Romans 8:35-39   I cannot be separated from the love of God

2 Corinthians 1:21   I have been established, anointed, and sealed by God

Colossians 3:3   I am hidden with Christ in God

Philippians 1:6	I am assured that the good work that God has started in me will be finished
Philippians 3:20	I am a citizen of heaven
2 Timothy 1:7	I have not been given a spirit of fear, but of power, love, and a sound mind
Hebrews 4:16	I can find grace and mercy in time of need
1 John 5:18	I am born of God and the evil one cannot touch me

I am significant:

Matthew 5:13	I am the salt and light for everyone around me
John 15:1,5	I am a part of the true vine, joined to Christ and able to produce much fruit
John 15:16	I have been handpicked by Jesus to bear fruit
Acts 1:8	I am a personal witness of Christ's
1 Corinthians 3:16	I am God's temple, where the Holy Spirit lives
2 Corinthians 5:17 20	I am at peace with God, and He has given me the work of making peace between Himself and other people—I am a minister of reconciliation
2 Corinthians 6:1	I am God's co-worker
Ephesians 2:6	I am seated with Christ in the heavenlies
Ephesians 2:10	I am God's workmanship

Ephesians 3:12   I may approach God with freedom
and confidence

Philippians 4:13   I can do all things through Christ
who strengthens me

There is no way we can fix our failures and sins of the past, but by the grace of God we can be free from them. God's Word declares, "If anyone is in Christ, he is a new creation; the old has gone, the new has come!" (2 Corinthians 5:17). Furthermore, we are seated with Christ in the heavenlies, far above Satan's authority (Ephesians 2:4-6; Colossians 2:10-11), which means we have the authority to do God's will. But we also have a responsibility. We must *believe the truth* of who we are in Christ and *change how we live* as children of God.

The major problem with those living in bondage—sexual or other—is that they do not *see* the truths shared above. So Paul prays "that the eyes of your heart may be enlightened in order that you may know the hope to which he has called you, the riches of his glorious inheritance in the saints, and his incomparably great power for us who believe" (Ephesians 1:18-19). We already share in Christ's rich inheritance, and we already have the power to live victoriously in Christ. God has already accomplished for us what we could not do for ourselves.

My prayer also is that the eyes of your heart will be opened to see the inheritance and power God has provided for you in Christ. As we go on in this chapter you will discover more of what you must *believe* in order to experience your freedom from sexual bondage. In the next chapter you will learn how to *walk* in accordance with that liberating truth.

Our Position in Christ

Paul argues in Romans 6:1-11 that what is true about Christ you should count as true about yourself also because you are alive "in Christ."* He also explains that if death has no mastery over us, then sin doesn't either.

---

* Paul further confirms this in 8:16-17: "The Spirit himself testifies with our spirit that we are God's children. Now if we are children, then we are heirs—heirs of God and coheirs with Christ."

When you read a command in the Bible, the only proper response is to obey it. When you find a promise in God's Word, you are to claim it. When Scripture is stating something that is true, the only proper response is for you to believe it. It's a simple concept, but many Christians try to do for themselves what Christ has already done for them. That should become clear as we discuss Paul's teaching below.

The New Testament Greek language appears to be more precise concerning verb tenses than our English language. You can know when a verb is past, present, or future tense, and whether the verb is describing continuous action or an action that occurred at a point in time. However, you don't have to know the Greek language to appreciate what the Word of God is saying. Though the English translations bring this out fairly well, it is helpful to know that the verb tenses in Romans 6:1-10 are all past tense. In other words, this truth has already happened—and the only way we appropriately respond is by faith.

You Are Dead to Sin

Paul starts this passage by asking, "What shall we say, then? Shall we go on sinning so that grace may increase? By no means! We died to sin; how can we live in it any longer?" (verses 1-2). The defeated or naïve Christian may ask, "How do I do that? How do I die to sin, including the sexual sins that have me bound?" The answer is, "You can't do it!" Why not? Because you have already died. You died to sin the moment you were born again. "We died to sin" is past tense. It has already happened for every child of God. This truth is something you must believe, not something you must do.

"I *can't* be dead to sin," you may respond, "because I don't *feel* dead to sin." You will have to set your feelings aside for a few verses, because it's what you believe that sets you free, not what you feel. God's Word is true whether you choose to believe it or not. Believing the Word of God doesn't make it true; His Word is true, therefore you must believe it even if your feelings don't match. That is not the same as denying your emotions, which is never healthy. I will explain in a later chapter the proper place for our emotions.

You Were Baptized into Christ's Death

Paul continues, "Don't you know that all of us who were baptized into Christ Jesus were baptized into his death?" (verse 3). Are you still wondering, *How do I do that?* The answer is the same: You can't do it, because you have *already* been baptized into Christ Jesus. It happened the moment you placed your faith in Jesus Christ as Savior and Lord. It is futile to seek something the Bible affirms that we already have: "We were all baptized by one Spirit into one body" (1 Corinthians 12:13). "We were" is past tense. It has already happened, therefore believe it.

This passage is addressing our spiritual baptism into Christ. Baptism as an ordinance or sacrament practiced by most churches is usually understood as an initiation rite. Augustine called the rite of baptism a "visible form of an invisible grace."

FAILING TO MAKE THE CONNECTION

A pastor shared with me, "I have been struggling for 22 years in my Christian experience. It's been one trial after another, and I think I have finally found the answer. I was doing my devotions the other day when I came across Colossians 3:3: 'You died, and your life is now hidden with Christ in God.' That's the key to victory, isn't it?" I assured him it was. Then he asked, "How do I do that?"

Surprised by his question, I asked him to look at the passage again and read it just a little more slowly. So he read it again: "'You died, and your life is hidden with Christ in God.'" Again he asked in desperation, "I know I need to die with Christ, but how do I do it?" This dear man had been desperately trying for 22 years to become someone he already is! He's not alone. Many Bible-believing Christians are bogged down in their Christian walk because they have failed to understand their identity and position in Christ.

You Were Raised to New Life in Christ

We were therefore buried with him through baptism into death in order that, just as Christ was raised from the dead through the glory of the Father, we too may live a new life. If we have been united with him like this in his death, we will certainly also be united with him in his resurrection (Romans 6:4-5).

Have we been united with Him? Absolutely! "If we have been united with him" is, grammatically, a *first-class conditional clause*. It can literally be read, "If we have become united with Him in the likeness of His death—and we certainly have—we shall also be united with Him in the likeness of His resurrection."

Paul argues that we cannot receive into our lives only part of Jesus. You cannot identify with the death and burial of Christ without also identifying with His resurrection and ascension. You will live in defeat if you believe only half the gospel. You have died with Christ, *and* you have been raised with Him and seated with Him in the heavenlies (Ephesians 2:6). From this position you have all the authority and power you need to live the Christian life. Every child of God is spiritually alive "in Christ" and is identified with Him:

- in His death (Romans 6:3,6; Galatians 2:20; Colossians 3:1-3)
- in His burial (Romans 6:4)
- in His resurrection (Romans 6:5,8,11)
- in His ascension (Ephesians 2:6)
- in His life (Romans 5:10-11)
- in His power (Ephesians 1:19-20)
- in His inheritance (Romans 8:16-17; Ephesians 1:11-12)

Jesus didn't come only to die for our sins; He also came to give us life (John 10:10). If all we understand is the crucifixion, then we will believe ourselves to be only "forgiven sinners" instead of redeemed saints—that is, *children of God*. We celebrate the resurrection of Jesus Christ on Easter, not just His death on Good Friday. It is the resurrected life of Christ that we are to abide in.

Notice how Paul unfolds this truth in Romans 5:8-11. "God demonstrates his own love for us in this: While we were still sinners, Christ died for us" (verse 8). Isn't that great, Christian? God loves you! But is that all? No! "Since we have now been justified by his blood, *how much more* shall we be saved from God's wrath through him!" (verse 9).

Isn't that great, Christian? You're not going to hell! But is that all? No! "For if, when we were God's enemies, we were reconciled to him through the death of his Son, *how much more,* having been reconciled, shall we be saved through his life!" (verse 10).

You are being saved by His life. Eternal life isn't something you get when you die. You are alive in Christ right now. What Adam and Eve lost in the fall was life—that is, eternal and spiritual life. But is that all? No! "Not only is this so, but we also rejoice in God through our Lord Jesus Christ, through whom we have now received reconciliation" (verse 11). This reconciliation assures us that our souls are in union with God, which is what it means to be spiritually alive.

Peter also affirms this incredible truth:

> His divine power has given us everything we need for life and godliness through our knowledge of him who called us by his own glory and goodness. Through these he has given us his very great and precious promises, so that through them you may participate in the divine nature and escape the corruption in the world caused by evil desires (2 Peter 1:3-4).

Are you beginning to see a glimmer of hope for overcoming sexual bondage? You should be, because you have already died to it and have been raised to new and victorious life in Christ.

Your Old Self Was Crucified with Christ

Paul continues in Romans 6, "We know that our old self was crucified with him so that the body of sin might be done away with, that we should no longer be slaves to sin" (6:6). The text does not say "we must do." It says, "we *know.*" Your old self was crucified with Christ. The only proper response to this powerful truth is to believe it.

Many people are desperately trying to put to death the old self, with all its tendencies to sin—but they can't do it. Why not? Because it is already dead! You cannot do for yourself what God alone can and already has done for you.

Christians who continually fail in their Christian experience begin to reason incorrectly and ask, "What experience must I undergo in order for me to live victoriously?" There is none. The only experience that is necessary for this verse to be true occurred over 2000 years ago on the cross. And the only way we can enter into that experience today is by faith. We can't save ourselves, and we can't overcome the penalty of death or the power of sin by human effort. Only God can do that for us, and He has already done it.

As I was explaining this truth during a conference, a man raised his hand and said, "I've been a Christian for 13 years. Why hasn't someone told me this before?" Maybe no one had shared with him, or maybe he hadn't been listening. Don't think that this is just "positional truth," which implies that there is little or no present-day benefit in being alive and free in Christ. This is not pie-in-the-sky theology. This is the only basis for our hope of ever living a righteous life. If we choose to believe it and live accordingly by faith, the truth of this passage will work itself out in our experience. Trying to make it true by our experience will lead to defeat.

We don't live obediently hoping that God may someday accept us. We are already accepted by God, so we live obediently. We don't labor in God's vineyard hoping that He may someday love us. God already loves us, so we joyfully labor in His vineyard. It is not what we do that determines who we are—it is who we are and what we believe that determines what we do.

You Have Been Freed from Sin

"Anyone who has died has been freed from sin" (Romans 6:7). Have you died with Christ? Then you are free from sin. You may be thinking, *I don't feel free from sin.* If you only believe what you feel, you will never live a victorious life. Most of us wake up some mornings feeling very alive to sin and very dead to Christ. But that's just the way we feel. If we believed what we feel and walked that way the rest of the day, what kind of a day do you think we would have? It would be a pretty bad day!

I have learned to greet each new day by praying, *Dear Lord, I deserved eternal damnation, but You gave me eternal life. I ask You to fill me with Your Holy Spirit, and I choose to walk by faith regardless of how I feel. I know I will face many temptations today, but I choose to take every thought captive to the obedience of Christ and to think upon that which is true and right.*

A seminary student asked me in class, "Are you telling me I don't have to sin?"

I responded, "Where did you get the idea you have to sin?" I quoted 1 John 2:1 to the class: "My dear children, I write this to you so that you will not sin. But if anybody does sin, we have one who speaks to the Father in our defense—Jesus Christ, the Righteous One." God does not refer to us in Scripture as sinners. We are clearly identified as saints who have the capacity to sin, and who will do so whenever they choose to walk by the flesh and believe lies.

Obviously, Christian maturity is a factor in our ability to stand against temptation, but what an incredible sense of defeat must accompany the belief that we are bound to sin when God commands us not to sin! Many people in sexual bondage are caught in this hopeless web. They think, *God, You made me this way—and now You condemn me for it. Unfair!* That would be unfair, but God didn't create Adam and Eve to be alive physically and dead spiritually. They chose to separate themselves from God by their own sin. We also have made choices to sin, and we will never recover unless we assume responsibility for our actions and attitudes.

God has done all He needs to do for us to live victorious lives in Christ. It is equally wrong to say, "The Christian life is impossible!" Then when those who say this fail, they proclaim, "I'm only human!" They believe the lie that the scope of the gospel isn't big enough to include sexual bondage. Such thinking reflects a faulty belief system.

We have been saved, not by how we *behave,* but by how we *believe.* This is a paradox and stumbling block to the natural mind. But to biblically informed Christians, it is the basis for our freedom and conquest—our union with God and our walk by faith.

There is no greater sin than the sin of unbelief. On more than one occasion the Lord made statements like "according to your faith will it be done to you" (Matthew 9:29). Paul wrote, "Everything that does not come from faith is sin" (Romans 14:23). If we choose to believe a lie, we will live a lie, but if we choose to believe the truth, we will live a victorious life by faith—that is, by the same means by which we were saved.

Death Is No Longer Your Master

"If we died with Christ, we believe that we will also live with him. For we know that since Christ was raised from the dead, he cannot die again; death no longer has mastery over him" (Romans 6:8-9). Does death have mastery over any believer? Absolutely not! Why? Because death could not master Christ, and you are alive in Him:

> "Death has been swallowed up in victory." "Where, O death, is your victory? Where, O death, is your sting?" The sting of death is sin, and the power of sin is the law. But thanks be to God! He gives us the victory through our Lord Jesus Christ (1 Corinthians 15:54-57).

Since Christ has triumphed over death by His resurrection, death has no mastery over us who are spiritually alive in Christ Jesus. Jesus said, "I am the resurrection and the life. He who believes in me will live [spiritually], even though he dies [physically]; and whoever lives and believes in me will never die [spiritually]. Do you believe this?" (John 11:25-26). Do you believe what Jesus said? Then be it done to you according to how you believe!

A Once-for-All Death

Paul continues, "The death he died, he died to sin once for all; but the life he lives, he lives to God" (Romans 6:10). This was accomplished when "God made him who had no sin to be sin for us, so that in him we might become the righteousness of God" (2 Corinthians 5:21). When Jesus went to the cross, when they nailed those spikes into His hands and feet, the Father was in the process of laying all the sins of the world upon Him. But when He was resurrected, there were no sins upon Him. They stayed in the grave. As He sits at the right hand of the Father today, there are no sins upon Him. Jesus has triumphed over sin and death. Since you are alive in Him, you are also dead to sin.

Many Christians accept the truth that Christ died for the sins they have already committed, but what about the sins they commit in the future? When Christ died for all your sins, how many of your sins were then future? All of them! This is not a license to sin, which is the basis for our addictions, but a marvelous truth on which to stand against Satan's accusations. It is the truth we must know in order to live free in Christ.

The One-Step Response

In Romans 6:11, Paul summarizes how we are to respond to what Christ has accomplished for us by His death and resurrection: "In the same way, count yourselves dead to sin but alive to God in Christ Jesus." We do not make ourselves dead to sin by considering it to be so. We consider ourselves dead to sin because God says it already is so. The King James version of the same verse reads, "Reckon yourselves to be dead unto sin." If you think that your reckoning makes you dead to sin, you will reckon yourself into a wreck! We can't make ourselves dead to sin; only God can do that—and He has already done it. Paul is saying we must keep on choosing to believe by faith what God says is true, even when our feelings say otherwise.

The verb "count" (or "reckon") is present tense. In other words, we must continuously believe this truth and daily affirm we are dead to sin and alive in Christ. This is essentially the same thing as abiding in Christ (John 15:1-8) and walking by the Spirit (Galatians 5:16). As we take our stand in the truth of what God has done and who we are in Christ, we will not easily be deceived or be led to carry out the desires of the flesh.

Living Under a Greater Law

Has sin disappeared because we have died to it? No. Has the power of sin diminished? No, it is still strong and still appealing. But when sin makes its appeal, we have the power and authority to say no to it because our relationship with sin ended when the Lord "rescued us from the dominion of darkness and brought us into the kingdom of the Son he loves" (Colossians 1:13).

Paul explains how this is possible in Romans 8:1-2: "There is now no condemnation for those who are in Christ Jesus, because through Christ Jesus the law of the Spirit of life set me free from the law of sin and death."

Is the law of sin and death still operative? Yes, and that is why Paul calls it a law, because a law cannot be done away with. It has been overcome by a greater law—"the law of the Spirit of life in Christ Jesus." To illustrate, can you fly by your own power? No, because the law of gravity keeps you bound to earth. But you *can* fly in an airplane, which has a power greater than the law of gravity. As long as you remain in the airplane you can fly. If you jump out at 20,000 feet and try flying on your own, you will crash and burn.

Like gravity, the law of sin and death is still here, still operative, still powerful, and still making its appeal. But you don't need to submit to it. The law of the Spirit of life is a greater law. As long as you live by the Spirit, you will not carry out the desires of the flesh (Galatians 5:16). You must "be strong in the Lord and in his mighty power" (Ephesians 6:10). The moment you think you can stand on your own, the moment you stop depending on the Lord, you are headed for a fall (Proverbs 16:18).

All temptation is an attempt by the devil to get us to live our lives independently of God. "So, if you think you are standing firm, be careful that you don't fall! No temptation has seized you except what is common to man. And God is faithful; he will not let you be tempted beyond what you can bear. But when you are tempted, he will also provide a way out so that you can stand up under it" (1 Corinthians 10:12-13). When we succumb to temptation and are deceived by the father of lies, we should quickly repent of our sin, renounce the lies, return to our loving Father—who cleanses us—and resume the walk of faith.

⊷═⊙═⊶

Perhaps you have struggled in defeat against sexual sin and bondage while vainly trying to figure out what you must do to get free. I hope the truth of Romans 6:1-11 has unlocked the prison doors in your understanding. It's not what you do that sets you free—it's what Christ has already done and what you are now choosing to believe. God has done everything that needs to be done through the death and resurrection of Jesus Christ. Your vital first step to freedom is to believe that, claim it, and stake your life on it.

QUESTIONS FOR DISCUSSION AND THOUGHT

1. Why can't we just stop sinning?

2. Salvation brings forgiveness of sins, but what else does it bring?

3. What did you think of yourself before salvation? What should you think of yourself after salvation?

4. Why do many Christians not know who they are in Christ? Do you know who you are in Christ? When did you discover that truth?

5. How can we fix the past things that we have done?

6. What can't we do that Christ has already done for us?

7. Why do you think many believers identify with Christ's death and not His resurrection?

8. Do we make something true by our experience? Or do we believe something to be true, and then it works out in our experience when we choose to live by faith? Explain that.

9. Is sin master over you? Why or why not?

10. How do you overcome the law of sin and the law of death?

6

OVERCOMING SIN'S ENTRAPMENT

It is absolutely certain that if a man sins, his own
sin will dog him, that it will keep on his track night
and day, like a bloodhound, and never quit until
it catches him and brings him to account.

R.A. TORREY

As with many victims, Melissa's memories of sexual abuse were blocked by the trauma she had experienced. However, her negative view of herself and abnormal childhood behavior signaled a deep, hidden problem, as we see from her story:

> I felt so inadequate and unacceptable as a child. I avoided getting close to anyone, especially boys, fearing they would find out how terrible I was. Everyone seemed to react to me in a sexual way. When I was a girl of six or seven, men whispered to me what they wanted to do to me when I got older. As I grew up, women seemed threatened by me, as if I intended to steal their husbands. This behavior only reinforced my belief there was something wrong with me and everyone saw it. I had become a Christian as a young child, but I was convinced God had picked me out to be sexually tormented and abused.
>
> About the time I turned nine or ten, I began to experiment with masturbation. I also became quite self-destructive. I cut the insides of my legs and put alcohol on the wounds to make them hurt more. I cut pieces of skin off my knuckles

just to feel the pain I knew I deserved. As a young teen I was shy and afraid of boys. I didn't have many friends. When I dated, I either froze up after a little bit of necking or blanked out, unable to remember what I did or how I got home. I became bulimic at about 14.

I rededicated my life to Christ at age 15. But as I left high school and entered college I continued to binge and purge once or twice a day. I also strayed into a few sexual involvements, and most of those guys were also Christians. I wanted to be loved and accepted, so I gave them my body. But when I did, the boys just used me and discarded me. With or without sex, the boys rejected me. I felt dirty and trapped.

When Melissa married Dan in her early twenties, their physical intimacy opened a floodgate of memories and nightmares about her clouded past. She dreamed about her grandfather raping her while her new husband watched with enjoyment. Gradually the repressed memories of her horrifying past came into focus.

She recalled being molested by her grandfather at age two. She was forced to accept and perform oral sex and other atrocities with him as a young child. At the time she was cutting herself, she was also awakened often in the middle of the night by severe abdominal pain. An insightful doctor told Melissa's mother that she was being sexually abused. The mother blamed Melissa's stepfather, brother, and uncle—everyone but her grandfather, the real culprit.

Melissa felt betrayed by the doctor for revealing her "secret." She had never considered telling anyone how Grandpa "loved" her, even though she felt it was wrong. She was confused. She loved her grandfather, but she also prayed that God would kill him to make the abuse stop. When he did die before Melissa became a teenager, she felt responsible and mourned him. But the inner wounds he had inflicted continued to torment her for years.

The Way Out of the Trap

Sexual abuse devastates the whole person. It distorts their worldview and their concept of God and themselves. Studies show that nearly half of all female children will experience some form of sexual abuse before they reach their fourteenth birthday.[6] Furthermore, the perpetrators of 85 to 94 percent of sexual violations are either relatives, family friends, neighbors, or acquaintances of the victim, not strangers.[7] The abused come to Christ, hear the truth—but they can't seem to appropriate it. Both the abused and the abuser are trapped in the "sin-confess-sin-confess-and-sin-again" cycle. In most cases they have failed to deal with sin's entrapment.

In the previous chapter we looked at Romans 6:1-11 and learned what Christ has already done for us. We have a responsibility as well, and Paul shares that in Romans 6:12-13. However, what God requires us to do in verses 12 and 13 will not be effective if we are not believing what Paul teaches in verses 1 through 11. *Truth sets us free* from the bondage of sin, and *believing the truth* precedes responsible behavior.

Give Yourself as an Offering

Based on his previous teaching in Romans 6, Paul assigns the following responsibility to all believers: "Therefore do not let sin reign in your mortal body so that you obey its evil desires" (verse 12). According to this verse, it is our responsibility to not allow sin to reign in our mortal bodies. We cannot say, "The devil made me do it," or that anyone else made us do it either. God never commands us to do something we cannot do, and the devil can't prevent us from doing it. In Christ, we have died to sin—and the devil can't *make* us do anything. He will tempt us, accuse us, and try to deceive us—but if sin reigns in our mortal body, it does so because *we* have allowed it. In order to live a liberated life in Christ we must assume responsibility for our own attitudes and actions.

How then do we prevent sin from reigning in our bodies? Paul answers in verse 13: "Do not offer the parts of your body to sin, as instruments of wickedness, but rather offer yourselves to God, as those who have been brought from death to life; and offer the parts of your body to him as instruments of righteousness." Notice that there is only one negative action to avoid, and two positive actions to practice.

Don't offer the parts of your body to sin. We are not to use our eyes, hands, feet, or any part of our bodies in any way that would serve sin. When you see a sexually explicit program on TV and lustfully watch it, you are offering your body to sin. When you get inappropriately "touchy-feely" with a co-worker of the opposite sex, you are offering your body to sin. When you fantasize sexually about someone other than your spouse, you are offering your body to sin. Whenever you choose to offer parts of your body to sin, you invite sin to rule in your physical body. "What is the source of quarrels and conflicts among you? Is not the source your pleasures that wage war in your members?" (James 4:1 NASB).

Offer yourself and the parts of your body to God. Notice that Paul makes a distinction between "yourselves" and "the parts of your body." What is the distinction? Self is who we are on the inside—the immaterial or inner person that is being renewed day by day (2 Corinthians 4:16). Our bodies and their various parts are who we are on the outside, the mortal, temporal part of us. Someday we are going to jettison our old "earth suits." At that time we will be absent from our mortal bodies and present with the Lord and receive immortal bodies (2 Corinthians 5:8). As long as we are on planet Earth, however, our inner selves are united with our outer physical bodies. We are to offer the complete package—body, soul, and spirit—to God.

Paul wrote, "The body that is sown is perishable, it is raised imperishable; it is sown in dishonor, it is raised in glory; it is sown in weakness, it is raised in power; it is sown a natural body, it is raised a spiritual body" (1 Corinthians 15:42-44). Our inner man will live forever with our heavenly Father, but our bodies won't. Paul continues: "Flesh and blood cannot inherit the kingdom of God, nor does the perishable inherit the imperishable" (verse 50). That which is mortal is corruptible.

Is our physical body evil? No, it's amoral, or neutral. So what are we to do about the neutral disposition of our bodies? We are instructed to present them to God "as instruments of righteousness." To "present" means to "place at the disposal of." An instrument can be anything the

Lord has entrusted to us, including our bodies. For example, your car is an amoral, neutral instrument for your use. You can use your car for good or bad purposes—you can choose to drive people to church or to sell drugs. Similarly, your body can be used for good or evil purposes as you choose. You have opportunities every day to offer your eyes, your hands, your brain, your feet, and so on, to sin or to God. The Lord commands us to be good stewards of our bodies and use them only as instruments of righteousness. Ultimately, it's our choice.

Your Body, God's Temple

In 1 Corinthians 6:13-20, Paul offers a little more body theology, especially as it relates to sexual immorality:

> The body is not meant for sexual immorality, but for the Lord, and the Lord for the body. By his power God raised the Lord from the dead, and he will raise us also. Do you not know that your bodies are members of Christ himself? Shall I then take the members of Christ and unite them with a prostitute?
>
> Never! Do you not know that he who unites himself with a prostitute is one with her in body? For it is said, "The two will become one flesh." But he who unites himself with the Lord is one with him in spirit.
>
> Flee from sexual immorality. All other sins a man commits are outside his body, but he who sins sexually sins against his own body. Do you not know that your body is a temple of the Holy Spirit, who is in you, whom you have received from God? You are not your own; you were bought at a price. Therefore honor God with your body.

This passage teaches that we have more than a spiritual union with God. Our bodies are members of Christ Himself. Romans 8:11 declares, "If the Spirit of him who raised Jesus from the dead is living in you, he who raised Christ from the dead will also give life to your mortal bodies through his Spirit, who lives in you." Our bodies are actually God's temple because His Spirit dwells in us. To use our bodies for sexual immorality is to defile the temple of God.

As a Christian, aren't you offended when people suggest that Jesus was sexually intimate with Mary Magdalene? Jesus was fully God, and He was also fully man. He was tempted in every way we are, including sexually, but He never sinned. His earthly body was not meant for sexual immorality, and neither is ours. If our eyes were fully open to the reality of the spiritual world and we understood the violation felt in heaven when we sin against our own bodies, we would more quickly obey the Scripture's command to flee from sexual immorality.

Can you think of any way you could commit a sexual sin and *not* be using your body as an instrument of unrighteousness? I can't. Therefore, when we do commit a sexual sin, we allow sin to reign in our mortal bodies! Are we still united with the Lord? Yes, because He will never leave us nor forsake us. We don't lose our salvation, but we certainly lose our daily victory.

KEEP YOURSELF FOR GOD

It is hard for us to fully understand the moral outrage felt in heaven when one of God's children uses His temple as an instrument of unrighteousness. It is even worse when someone defiles the temple of another person through rape or incest. It compares to the despicable act of Antiochus Epiphanes in the second century before Christ. This godless Syrian ruler overran Jerusalem, declared the Mosaic ceremonies illegal, erected a statue of Zeus in the Temple, and slaughtered a pig—an unclean animal—on the altar. Can you imagine how God's people must have felt to have their holy place so thoroughly desecrated? Have you ever felt the same way about defiling God's temple, which is our bodies?

Paul urges us, "You were called to freedom, brethren; only do not turn your freedom into an opportunity for the flesh, but through love serve one another" (Galatians 5:13 NASB).

An Immoral Bond

What happens when a child of God—who is united with the Lord and one spirit with Him—also "unites himself with a prostitute" through sexual immorality? The Bible says they become one flesh. They bond together. I can't fully explain it, but I have certainly seen it. Bonding is a positive thing in a wholesome relationship, but in an immoral union, bonding only leads to bondage.

How many times have you heard of an upright Christian young woman who becomes involved with an immoral man, has sex with him, and then continues in a sick relationship with him? He may mistreat her, and friends and relatives tell her, "He's no good for you. Get rid of the bum!" But she won't listen to them. Even though he treats her badly, the woman won't leave him. Why? Because a spiritual and emotional bond has been formed. The two of them have become one flesh. Such bonds must be broken in Christ.

This spiritual and emotional bond can occur as a result of heavy petting or oral sex. At a conference, a colleague and I counseled a young husband and wife who were experiencing marital problems. Even though they were committed to each other, their sexual relationship had been dull and lifeless since their wedding. Both husband and wife had been romantically involved before marriage with other partners, though without intercourse.

During our counseling session, both husband and wife admitted for the first time that they were still emotionally attached to their "first loves." At our encouragement, they renounced petting and romantic involvement with their previous partners and recommitted their lives and their bodies to the Lord. They further committed to reserve the sexual use of their bodies for each other only. The next day they shared with me that they had a joyful, intimate encounter with each other that night—a first for their marriage. Once the sexual and emotional bonds had been broken, they were free to enjoy each other the way God intended.

In the Steps to Freedom in Christ, we encourage the people we counsel to pray and ask the Lord to reveal every sexual use of their bodies as instruments of unrighteousness—and God does. Then for each one God brings to mind, they pray, "I renounce that use of my body (having sex) with (the person's name), and I ask you to break that sexual bond." If there has been an emotional attachment, they pray, "...break that sexual and emotional bond." Then they are urged to give their bodies to God as living sacrifices and pray that God would fill them with His Holy Spirit. Finally, they are encouraged to forgive those who have offended them. They forgive others for their own sakes, since nothing will keep them more bound to their past than unforgiveness. To forgive is to set a captive free and then realize you were the captive.

I mentioned earlier that in the cases of rape and incest, a person's temple is also defiled, even though they are innocent. "Not fair!" you say. Of course it isn't fair—it is a violation of that person's temple, just like Antiochus Epiphanes' violation of the Jewish Temple...and those who tried to stop him were martyred. People who have been victimized don't have to remain victims. They can renounce that use of their body and give it to God as a living sacrifice. Freedom comes when they have forgiven their abuser and have let God be the avenger.

I was asked by a local pastor to counsel a young lady who was hearing voices in her head. They were so audible to her that she couldn't understand why we couldn't hear them. She had lived with a man who had abused her and dealt drugs for a living. She was now living at home but was still attached to him. Near the beginning of the session I asked her what she would do if we asked her to make a commitment to never see him again. She said, "I would probably get up and leave." I suspected that would be the case, but I wanted the pastor to hear it, and I want you to hear it. Having her make such a commitment was a legitimate goal, but the timing was wrong.

After hearing her story, I asked if she would like to resolve the problems she was having in her life. She wholeheartedly agreed, and I led her through the Steps. When we were done, there were no more demonic voices in her head, and she seemed to be in complete peace.

Finally she remarked, "I am never going to see that man again." That conviction had come from God, but it hadn't come until she had fully repented. Trying to get other people, such as our children, to make behavioral changes without inner conviction won't work.

Offering Yourself to God

Wonderful things happen when we determine to offer our bodies to God as instruments of righteousness instead of offering our bodies to sin. The Old Testament sacrificial system under the law was a picture of things to come. The sin offering in the Old Testament was a blood offering. Blood was drained from the sacrificial animal, and the carcass was taken outside the camp and disposed of. Only the blood was offered to God for the forgiveness of sin. Hebrews 9:22 states, "Without the shedding of blood there is no forgiveness."

At the cross, the Lord Jesus Christ became our sin offering. After He shed His blood for us, His body was taken down and buried outside the city, but unlike the slain lamb of the Old Testament, the Lamb of God did not stay buried for long.

The other primary offering in the Old Testament was a burnt offering. Unlike the sin offering, the burnt offering was totally consumed on the altar—blood, carcass, everything. In the Hebrew language, *burnt* literally means "that which ascends." In the burnt offering, the whole sacrificial animal ascended to God in flames and smoke from the altar. It was "an aroma pleasing to the LORD" (Leviticus 1:9).

Jesus is the sin offering, but who is the burnt offering? We are! Paul writes, "I urge you, brothers, in view of God's mercy, to offer your bodies as living sacrifices, holy and pleasing to God—this is your spiritual act of worship" (Romans 12:1). It's wonderful to know that our sins are forgiven; Christ did that for us when He shed His blood. But if you want to live victoriously in Christ over the sin that plagues you, you must present yourself to God and present your body as an instrument of righteousness. Such a sacrifice is "pleasing to God," as the aroma of the burnt offering was in the Old Testament.

To illustrate this, consider the spiritual revival under King Hezekiah, as recorded in 2 Chronicles 29. First, Hezekiah cleaned out the temple and prepared it for worship by purifying it. This is a picture of repentance. Under the New Covenant believers are the temple of God. Second, the king consecrated the priests. In the New Testament, every child of God is part of the priesthood of believers. This also parallels Paul's instruction to present ourselves to God. Third, Hezekiah ordered the blood offering for the forgiveness of sins. Nothing visible happened during the blood offering, but according to God's law, the sins of the people were forgiven. Then "Hezekiah gave the order to sacrifice the burnt offering on the altar. As the offering began, singing to the LORD began also...All this continued until the sacrifice of the burnt offering was completed" (verses 27-28). The burnt offering was such a significant and worshipful event that it was surrounded by music in the temple. The account concludes, "Hezekiah and all the people rejoiced at what God had brought about for his people" (verse 36). Great joy results when believers obediently and wholeheartedly present themselves and their bodies to God.

It is not enough to have our sins forgiven—we must be filled with God's Holy Spirit. Notice what happens when we are filled, according to Ephesians 5:18-20:

> Do not get drunk on wine, which leads to debauchery. Instead, be filled with the Spirit. Speak to one another with psalms, hymns and spiritual songs. Sing and make music in your heart to the Lord, always giving thanks to God the Father for everything.

Just as in the Old Testament, music fills the temple when we yield ourselves to God.

Winning the Struggle with Sin

The music inside sexually bound Christians sounds more like a funeral dirge than a song of joy. They feel defeated instead of victorious. They have offered their bodies as instruments of sexual sin and feel hopelessly trapped in sexual bondage. They may experience occasional periods of relief and success at saying no to temptation—but sin is reigning in their mortal bodies, and they can't seem to get out of the sin-confess-and-sin-again cycle. Perhaps you find yourself in this discouraging condition.

Paul describes this struggle in Romans 7:15-25. The conversation that follows is based on many counseling sessions I have had with Christians struggling with temptation, sin, and bondage. You may find yourself identifying with Dan as I talk him through Paul's teaching. I trust you will also identify with the liberating truth of God's Word.[8]

Dan: Neil, I can't keep going on like this. I have been sexually promiscuous in the past, and I'm really sorry about it. I have confessed it to the Lord, but I can't seem to get victory over it. I commit myself to avoid pornography. But the temptation is overwhelming and I give in to it. I don't want to live like this! It's ruining my marriage.

Neil: Dan, let's look at a passage of Scripture that seems to describe what you are experiencing. Romans 7:15 reads, "What I am doing, I do not understand; for I am not practicing what I would like to do, but I am doing the very thing I hate." Would you say that pretty well describes your life?

Dan: Exactly! I really want to do what God says is right, and I hate being in bondage to this lust. I sneak down at night and call one of those sex hotlines, or I turn on my computer and get on the Internet. Afterward I feel disgusted with myself.

Neil: It sounds like you would identify with verse 16 as well: "But if I do the very thing I do not want to do, I agree with the Law, confessing that the Law is good." Dan, how many persons are mentioned in this verse?

Dan: There is only one person, and it is clearly "I."

Neil: It can be very defeating to know what we want to do, but for some reason not be able to do it. How have you tried to resolve this conflict?

Dan: Sometimes I wonder if I'm even a Christian. It seems to work for others but not for me. I sometimes doubt if the Christian life is possible or if God is really here.

Neil: You're not alone, Dan. Many Christians believe they are different from others, and most think they are the only ones who struggle with sexual temptations. If you were the only player in this battle, it would stand to reason that you would question your salvation or the existence of God. But look at verse 17: "So now, no longer am I the one doing it, but sin which dwells in me." Now how many players are there?

Dan: Apparently two, "I" and "sin." But I don't understand. Aren't *I* and *sin* the same?

Neil: Sometimes we *feel* like sin, but *we* are not sin. The Bible teaches that if we say we have no sin, we deceive ourselves (1 John 1:8). But *having* sin and *being* sin are two totally different issues. Now let's read verse 18 and see if we can make some sense out of it: "I know that nothing good dwells in me, that is, in my flesh; for the willing is present in me, but the doing of the good is not."

Dan: I learned that verse a long time ago. It's been easy for me to figure out that I'm no good for myself and no good for my wife. Sometimes I think it would be better if I just weren't here.

Neil: That's not true, because that's not what the verse says. In fact, it says the opposite. The "nothing good" that is dwelling in you is not *you.* It's something else. If I had a wood splinter in my finger, it would be "nothing good" dwelling in me. But the "nothing good" isn't me; it's a splinter. It's important to note that the "nothing good" is not even my flesh—rather, it is operating *in* my flesh ("sin nature"). If we see only ourselves in this struggle, living righteously will seem hopeless. This passage is going to great lengths to tell us there is a second party involved in our struggle, whose nature is evil and different from ours.

You see, Dan, when you and I were born, we were born under the penalty of sin. And we know that Satan and his emissaries are always working to keep us under that penalty. When God saved us, Satan lost that battle, but he didn't curl up his tail or pull in his fangs. He is now committed to keeping us under the power of sin. But in Christ we have died to sin and are no longer under its power.

In 1 John 2:12-14, the apostle John writes to little children because their sins are forgiven. In other words, they have overcome the penalty of sin. He writes to young men because they have overcome the evil one. In other words, they have overcome the power of sin. We have the authority in Christ to experience our victory over the penalty and power of sin, despite Satan's lies to the contrary. Romans 7 also says that this evil is going to work through the flesh, which remains with us after our salvation. It is our responsibility to crucify the flesh and to resist the devil.

Let's continue in the passage to see if we can learn more about how the battle is being waged. Verses 19-21 state, "For the good that I want, I do not do; but I practice the very evil that I do not want. But if I am doing the very thing I do not want, I am no longer the one doing it, but sin which dwells in me. I find then the principle that evil is present in me, the one who wants to do good."

Dan, can you identify from these verses the nature of the "nothing good" that dwells in you?

Dan: Sure, it is clearly evil and sin. But isn't it just my own sin? When I sin, I feel guilty.

Neil: There's no question that you and I sin, but we are not "sin" as such. Evil is present in us, but Paul is not calling us evil. In fact, he is making a clear distinction between *us* and the sin that is dwelling *in* us. This does not excuse us from sinning, because Paul wrote in Romans 6:12 that we are responsible not to let sin reign in our mortal bodies.

Dan, let me share another example of this passage. Consider those who struggle with eating disorders. Many of them cut themselves, force themselves to defecate, and binge and purge. They do this because they believe there is evil present in them, and they are trying to get it out. But cutting themselves or defecating or purging won't get rid of this kind of evil. The lies they have believed are exposed when they renounce defecating or purging or cutting themselves as a means of cleansing themselves, and trust only in the cleansing work of Christ. When you came under conviction about your sexual sin, what did you do?

Dan: I confessed it to God.

Neil: Dan, confession literally means "to agree with God." It is the same thing as walking in the light, or living in moral agreement with Him about our present condition. We must confess our sin if we are going to live in harmony with our heavenly Father, but that doesn't go far enough. Confession is only the first step to repentance. The man that Paul is writing about agrees with God that what he is doing is wrong, but that doesn't resolve his problem. You have confessed your sin to God, but you are still in bondage to lust. It has to be very frustrating for you. Have you ever felt so defeated that you want to lash out at someone or at yourself?

Dan: Almost every day!

Neil: But when you cool down, do you again entertain thoughts that are in line with who you really are as a child of God?

Dan: Always, and then I feel terrible about lashing out.

Neil: Verse 22 explains why: "For I joyfully concur with the law of God in the inner man." When we act out of character with who we really are, the Holy Spirit immediately brings conviction because of our union with God. Out of frustration and failure, we think or say things like "I'm not going back to church anymore." "Christianity doesn't work." "It was God who made me this way, and now I feel condemned all the time." "God promised to provide a way of escape. Well, where is it? I haven't found it!" But soon our true nature begins to express itself: "I know what I'm doing is wrong, and I know God loves me—but I'm so frustrated by my continuing failure."

Dan: Someone told me once that this passage was talking about a non-Christian.

Neil: There are some people who take that position, but it doesn't make sense to me. Does a natural man joyfully concur with the law of God in the inner man? Does an unbeliever agree with the law of God and confess that it is good? I don't think so! In fact, they speak out rather strongly against it. Some even hate us Christians for upholding such a moral standard. In reference to the person Paul describes in Romans chapter 7, every disposition of the heart is toward God including the mind, the emotions, and the will. That is not true for a natural man.

Now look at verse 23, which describes the nature of this battle with sin: "But I see a different law in the members of my body, waging war against the law of my mind and making me a prisoner of the law of sin which is in my members." According to this passage, Dan, where is the battle being fought?

Dan: The battle appears to be in the mind.

Neil: That's precisely where the battle rages. Now if Satan can get you to think you are the only one in the battle, you will get down on yourself or God when you sin, which is counterproductive to resolving the problem. Let me put it this way: Suppose you opened a door you were told not to open, and a dog came through the door and wrapped his teeth around your leg. Would you beat on yourself, or would you beat on the dog?

Dan: I suppose I would beat on the dog.

Neil: Of course you would. On the other side of the door, the "dog" is tempting you with thoughts like "Come on, open the door. I have an exciting video to show you." "Everybody else is doing it. You'll get away with it." So you open the door, and the dog comes in and grabs hold of your leg. You feel the pain of conviction as soon as you open the door, because the devil changes roles from tempter to accuser. Your mind is pummeled by his accusations: "You opened the door. You're a miserable excuse for a Christian. God certainly can't love someone as sinful as you."

So you cry out, "God, forgive me!" He does—actually, you are *already* forgiven. But the dog is still clinging to your leg! You are stuck in the cycle of sin-confess-sin-confess-sin-confess. You beat on yourself continually for your repeated failure.

People eventually get tired of beating on themselves, so they walk away from God under a cloud of defeat and condemnation. Paul expressed this feeling in verse 24: "Wretched man that I am! Who will set me free from the body of this death?" He doesn't say he's wicked or sinful, but that he's miserable. This man is not experiencing his freedom. His attempts to do the right thing are met with moral failure because he has submitted to God but has not resisted the devil (James 4:7). There is nobody more miserable than someone who knows what is right and wants to do what is right—but can't seem to do it.

Dan: That's me—miserable!

Neil: Wait a minute, Dan. There is victory. Jesus will set us free.

Look at verse 25: "Thanks be to God through Jesus Christ our Lord! So then, on the one hand I myself with my mind am serving the law of God, but on the other, with my flesh the law of sin." Let's go back to the dog illustration. Why isn't crying out to God enough to solve your ongoing conflict with sexual sin?

Dan: Well, like you said, the dog is still there. I guess I have to chase off the dog.

Neil: And you will also have to close the door. That means you get rid of all your pornography and cut off any future supply, including the Internet. If you have a sexual partner other than your wife, you must call her right now and tell her it's over.

Dan: But I owe her an explanation or something. I'll just meet with her once, and that will be that.

Neil: That won't work, Dan. If you go over to her house, you will end up in bed again. You need to call her right now in my presence and commit yourself to never see or contact her again. You owe your wife and no one else.

Dan: Okay, give me the phone...

◄─═◎ ◎═─►

Neil: Now that you've dealt with that relationship, here are the steps you must take:

First, realize that you are already forgiven. Christ died once for all your sins. You were right in confessing your sin to God because you need to own up to the fact that you opened the door when you knew it was wrong.

Second, to make sure that every door is closed, you need to ask the Lord to reveal to your mind every sexual use of your body as an instrument of unrighteousness. As the Lord brings them to your mind, renounce every sexual relationship you have had with another woman, and ask God to break that sexual and emotional bond. Your body belongs to God and it is not to be used for sexual immorality.

Third, present your body to God as a living sacrifice and reserve the sexual use of your body for your spouse only.

Finally, resist the devil, and he will flee from you.

Dan: I think I'm getting the picture. But *every* sexual use of my body! That will take a long time. Well, even if it takes a couple of hours, I guess it will be a lot easier than living in bondage for the rest of my life. I've been condemning myself for my inability to live the Christian life. I can also see why I have been questioning my salvation. I think I see it now—though Paul was frustrated about his failure, he didn't get down on himself. He accepted his responsibility. More important, he expressed confidence by turning to God, because the Lord Jesus Christ would enable him to live above sin.

Neil: You're on the right track. Condemning yourself won't help because there is no condemnation for those who are in Christ Jesus (Romans 8:1). We don't want to assist the devil in his role as the accuser. Most people who are in bondage question their salvation. I have counseled hundreds of people who have shared with me their doubts about God and themselves. Ironically, the very fact that they are sick of their sin and want to get out of it is one of the biggest assurances of their salvation. Non-Christians don't have those kinds of convictions.

There is one more important thing you need to know: No one particular sin, including sexual sin, is isolated from the rest of your life and the rest of reality. To gain complete freedom, you need to walk through all the Steps to Freedom in Christ. There are other issues that may be keeping you from having an intimate relationship with God such as occult involvement, deception, unforgiveness, pride, and rebellion. We will help you resolve those issues as well in a non-condemning way. Finally, you need to understand the battle that is going on for your mind, and that is what we will discuss next.

QUESTIONS FOR DISCUSSION AND THOUGHT

1. Why are so many people reluctant to report suffering sexual abuse when the abuser is a relative?

2. What are some ways (sexual and otherwise) that we can use our bodies as instruments of unrighteousness?

3. What happens when we do use our bodies as instruments of unrighteousness?

4. What is the difference between "ourselves" and "our bodies"?

5. What happens between you and a sexual partner when the sexual union is outside the will of God?

6. How can you violate the temple of God?

7. Why is it counterproductive to ask Christians to commit to behavioral standards without first resolving their internal personal and spiritual conflicts with God?

8. What is the difference between the sin offering and the burnt offering?

9. What part of the discussion on Romans 7:15-25 struck a chord with you? Why?

10. For the sake of complete resolution, why do we need to consider more than just our sexual sins?

7

WINNING THE
BATTLE FOR
YOUR MIND

The sins of the mind are the last habitation of the devil.

JAROL JOHNSON

S uppose you have worked most of your adult life for the same boss—a cantankerous, unreasonable tyrant. The man is known throughout the company for bursting into employees' offices and verbally abusing them for even the slightest error or discrepancy. You learned early during your employment to walk silently around the old grouch and avoid him as much as possible. Every time he appears at your door, you cringe in fear.

One day you arrive at work to learn that the old tyrant has been transferred to another branch. You are no longer under his authority, and your relationship with him has ended. Your new boss is mild-mannered, kind, considerate, and affirming. He has the best interests of his employees at heart. But you don't know that at first, so when you see your new boss coming down the hall, you start looking for a place to hide, just like you did around the old boss. When he steps into your office, your heart starts beating faster. You wonder what you're going to get reamed out for this time. Over time you get to know your new boss a little better, and your response to him changes. But it will take time to get to know him and to change your attitudes and actions toward him.

Old habits are hard to break. The more we are conditioned to a certain stimulus–response pattern, the more difficult it is to reprogram our minds. This is certainly true of established sexual thought patterns and habits that are contrary to God's Word. For many people, these flesh patterns, or mental strongholds, were ingrained in their minds long before they became Christians.

Breaking the Strongholds Is Possible

Can strongholds of sexual bondage in the mind be broken? Yes! If our minds have been programmed wrongly, they can be reprogrammed. If we have been conformed to this world, we can be transformed. If we learned something the wrong way, we can learn it the right way. Will this take time? Yes, it will take the rest of our lives to renew our minds and to develop our character. We will never be perfect in our understanding on this earth, nor will our character be perfect like Christ's, but this is what we pursue.

As we set about demolishing sexual strongholds in our mind, we

---

REPENTANCE BRINGS GROWTH

Christian maturity cannot fully take place unless Christians are firmly rooted in Christ. When people aren't experiencing their freedom in Christ they go from book to book, from pastor to pastor, and from counselor to counselor, but nothing seems to get resolved. It is amazing how fast they can grow, however, when they have genuinely repented and put their hope and trust in God.

After I had the privilege of helping a missionary find her freedom in Christ, she wrote,

> I'm firmly convinced of the significant benefits of finding our freedom in Christ. I was making some progress in therapy, but there is no comparison with the steps I am able to make now. My ability to "process" things has increased manyfold. Not only is my spirit more serene, my head is actually clearer! It's easier to make connections now. It seems like everything is easier to understand now.

are not just up against the world—the godless system we were raised in. And we are not just up against the flesh—including those preprogrammed habit patterns of thought that have been burned into our minds over time or by intense traumatic experiences. We're up against the world and the devil as well. All three influences are at work to turn our minds away from the truth and set us on a path to sexual bondage.

We still live in a fallen world. Television programs will never be totally cleaned up. Work places may display pornography, and people will use the Lord's name in vain. The world's influence is all around us. When Paul identified himself more with Christ and less with the world, he was able to say, "May I never boast except in the cross of our Lord Jesus Christ, through which the world has been crucified to me, and I to the world" (Galatians 6:14). We must consider ourselves dead to a world system that is in opposition to God's truth and sexual purity.

Christians still retain flesh patterns after salvation, but as we bond to Christ we also crucify the flesh: "Those who belong to Christ Jesus have crucified the flesh with its passions and desires. Since we live by the Spirit, let us keep in step with the Spirit" (Galatians 5:24-25). Satan still rules over this fallen world, but we are alive in Christ and dead to sin. When we resist the devil he will flee from us (James 4:7).

A Process of Adjustment

In chapter 5, we learned from Romans chapter 6 that we are no longer under the authority of sin and Satan because our relationship with sin has been severed. We are new creatures in Christ (2 Corinthians 5:17). Old flesh patterns and habits don't automatically go away, however. They are still ingrained in our minds after salvation. Traumatic memories of abuse during childhood may still cause us to recoil in pain. We have a new boss—Jesus Christ—but having lived under the domination of sin and Satan, we must adjust to the freedom our new Master has provided for us.

In Romans 6, Paul instructed us to believe that our relationship with God has set us free from our relationship with sin and death (verses 1-11). Then he challenged us to present ourselves and our bodies to God as instruments of righteousness (verses 12-13; 12:1). Knowing and doing this makes possible the next instruction:

> Do not conform any longer to the pattern of this world, but be transformed by the renewing of your mind. Then you will be able to test and approve what God's will is—his good, pleasing and perfect will (Romans 12:2).

In summary, here is what we have learned so far about overcoming sexual strongholds:

1. We have to know and choose to believe our identity and position in Christ—that we are alive in Christ and dead to sin. We have to know the truth that sets us free. This is the essential foundation for Christian living, because no one can consistently live in a way that is inconsistent with what they believe about themselves and God. What we do doesn't determine who we are. Who we are and what we believe about God and ourselves determines what we do.

2. We have to repent of our sins. For sexual sins, that includes renouncing every sexual use of our bodies as instruments of unrighteousness and presenting them to God as instruments of righteousness. Genuine repentance is accomplished by submitting to God and resisting the devil, as we see in James 4:7. This is what the Steps to Freedom in Christ are intended to accomplish.

3. We have to be transformed by the renewing of our minds.

Renewing Our Minds

In chapter 4, we noted that everything programmed into our memory banks before Christ is still there after salvation. Our brains recorded every experience we ever had, good and bad. Nobody pushed the "clear" button. The good news—literally, the gospel—is that we have all the resources we need to renew our minds. The Lord has sent us the Holy Spirit, who is the Spirit of truth (John 14:16-17), and He will guide us into all truth (John 16:13). Because we are alive in Christ, "we have the mind of Christ" (1 Corinthians 2:16). We have superior weapons to win the battle for our minds. Paul wrote,

> Though we live in the world, we do not wage war as the world does. The weapons we fight with are not the weapons of the world. On the contrary, they have divine power to demolish strongholds. We demolish arguments and every pretension that sets itself up against the knowledge of God, and we take captive every thought to make it obedient to Christ (2 Corinthians 10:3-5).

Paul is not talking about defensive armor. He is talking about battering-ram weaponry that tears down strongholds in our minds that have been raised up against the knowledge of God.

Practice "Threshold Thinking"

Paul also wrote that "no temptation has seized you except what is common to man. And God is faithful; he will not let you be tempted beyond what you can bear. But when you are tempted, he will also provide a way out so that you can stand up under it" (1 Corinthians 10:13). If we are going to take the "way out" God has provided for us, we must avail ourselves of God's provision and change how we respond at the threshold of every sexually tempting thought. We must take those first thoughts captive and make them obedient to Christ. If we allow ourselves to ruminate on tempting thoughts, we will eventually act on them.

For example, suppose a man is struggling with lust. One night his wife asks him to go to the store for milk. When he gets into the car, he wonders which store he should go to. He knows of a local convenience store that has a display of pornographic magazines. He can also buy milk at a grocery store, which is a safe environment. But the memory of the seductive photos he has ogled before at the convenience store gives rise to a tempting thought. The more he thinks about it, the harder it is to resist. When he pulls out of the driveway, he heads for the convenience store.

He has already lost the battle for his mind. In first-person-singular language the tempter is beckoning him: *Go ahead and take a peek—you know you want to. Everybody does it. You'll get away with it. Who would know?* On the way to the convenience store, all kinds of rationalizing thoughts cross his mind. He prays, *Lord, if You don't want me to look at the pornography, have my pastor be in the store buying milk, or close the store before I get there.* Since the store is open (do you know of any convenience stores that close in the evening?) and since his pastor isn't there, he takes a look. Our flesh has an incredible propensity to rationalize, which is why tempting thoughts must be stopped the moment we first encounter them.

But the man's stolen pleasure doesn't last. Even before he leaves the store, guilt and shame overwhelm him. The devil has changed his role from tempter to accuser: *You sicko. How can you call yourself a Christian? You're pathetic!* "Why did I do it?" he moans. He did it primarily because he ignored the way out that God made available to him before he even pulled out of the driveway. He failed to take that initial thought captive and make it obedient to Christ. Rare is the person who can turn away from sin once the initial tempting thought has been embraced.

Understanding How We Function

To gain a better understanding of sexual temptation and mental strongholds, we need to know how our outer (material) body relates to our inner (immaterial) soul or spirit (2 Corinthians 4:16). Our brain is part of our physical body. Our mind is part of our soul. There is a fundamental difference between our brain and our mind. When we die physically, our soul is separated from our body and our brain returns to dust. We will be present with the Lord and in our right minds.

The material and immaterial function together as shown in the following diagram.

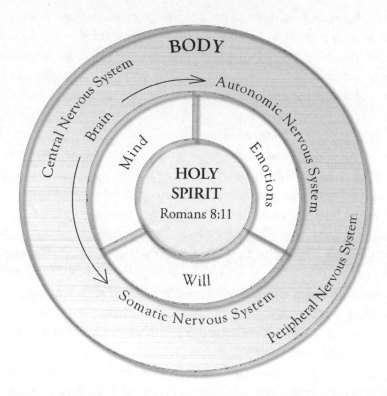

The primary correlation is between the mind and the brain. Our brain functions much like a digital computer. Neurons (brain cells) operate like little switches that turn on and off. Each neuron has many inputs—called dendrites—and only one output, which channels neurotransmitters to dendrites of other neurons. Millions of these connections make up the hardware of our brain. There are approximately 40 different types of neurotransmitters, of which serotonin and dopamine are the ones we hear the most about. Only 5 percent of our neurotransmitters are in our brain—the rest are carrying signals throughout our body.

Our mind functions much like computer software. As our brain receives input from the external world through the five senses, our mind compiles, analyzes, and interprets the data and chooses responses based on how it has been programmed. Our brain can't function in any way other than how our mind is programmed. As we have discussed, before we came to Christ, our minds were programmed by inputs from the world, the god of this world, and by the choices we made without the benefit of knowing God and His ways. Every pornographic image and every sexual experience is still stored in our memories.

Programming Problems

Many in the Western medical world tend to assume that mental and emotional problems are primarily caused by the hardware. There is no doubt that organic brain syndrome, Alzheimer's disease, and chemical imbalances can affect our ability to function mentally. The best program (mind) won't work if the computer (brain) is unplugged or in disrepair. However, the Christian's struggle with sin and bondage is not primarily a hardware problem, but a software problem. Renewing our mind is the process of reprogramming the software.

The brain and the spinal cord make up the central nervous system, which splits off into a peripheral nervous system comprised of two channels: the *somatic* and the *autonomic*. The somatic nervous system regulates large and small muscular movements, over which we have volitional control. That is why we can consciously and volitionally move an arm, a leg, or a toe. The somatic nervous system obviously correlates with our will.

The autonomic system regulates our glands, over which we have no volitional control. We don't tell our heart to beat or our glands to secrete hormones into our bloodstream. The autonomic nervous system correlates with our emotions, which we don't have volitional control over either. You cannot will yourself to change how you feel, but you can change how you think, which affects how you feel.

Sex glands are part of the autonomic nervous system. For instance, women have no volitional control over their menstrual cycles, and men have no volitional control over erections that occur during sleep. This is just the way God created our outer selves to operate.

If we have no control over our sex glands, then how can God expect us to have sexual self-control? Self-control is a fruit of the Spirit and a function of the inner self. Our sex glands are not the cause of sexual immorality; they just operate based on how our mind is programmed. Sexual behavior is determined by our thought life, and we *do* have control over what we think. If you fill your mind with pornography, you will drive your autonomic nervous system into the stops. Your sex glands will be set in motion, and you will likely behave in ways you will later regret. Just like a computer: If we put garbage in, we will get garbage out!

The Power of Visual Stimulation

Have you ever wondered why it is so hard to remember some things and to forget others? In school we study all night and then pray the facts won't leave our mind before we take the exam. One glance at a pornographic image, however, and it seems to stay in our mind for months and years. Why is that?

When we are stimulated emotionally—which includes being visually stimulated by sexual images—a signal is sent to our glands. A hormone called epinephrine is secreted into the bloodstream, which locks into our memory whatever stimulus is present at the time of the emotional excitement. This reaction causes us to involuntarily remember emotionally charged events—negative and traumatic ones as well as positive ones. It's too bad we don't get more emotionally excited about some of our subjects in school. We would remember them better!

Three viewings of hard-core pornography have the same lasting effect on us as an actual sexual experience. A person can become emotionally excited and sexually stimulated just from entertaining sexual thoughts. That's why an aroused man or woman will experience an emotional rush before any sexual contact is made. The man going to the convenience store where they sold pornography was sexually stimulated long before he even saw the magazines. The process begins in our thoughts, which trigger our autonomic nervous system, which secretes epinephrine into our bloodstream, which loads the image into our memory.

Emotions Are Products of Our Thoughts

Just as we can't volitionally control our glands, we can't directly control our emotions. If you think you can, try liking someone right now whom you don't like! We can't command our emotions that way, nor are there any instructions in Scripture for us to do so. We must acknowledge our emotions, however, because we can't be right with God if we aren't real about how we feel. Though we can't tell ourselves not to feel a certain way and can only acknowledge or deny how we feel, we do have control over how we think, and how we think controls how we feel. Scripture *does* tell us to control our thinking: "Brothers, stop thinking like children. In regard to evil be infants, but in your thinking be adults" (1 Corinthians 14:20).

This line of reasoning is the basis for cognitive therapy. People are doing what they're doing and feeling what they're feeling because of what they have chosen to think or believe. Therefore, we should try to change what we think or believe if we want to change our behavior or feelings. When applied from a Christian perspective, cognitive therapy is very close to repentance, which literally means "a change of mind."

If what we choose to believe does not reflect truth, then what we feel will not conform to reality. Let me illustrate. Suppose a man has been working for many years at a company that is now downsizing. People are getting laid off, but he thinks he is secure. Then one Monday morning he gets a note from his boss telling him that he wants to see him Friday at 10:00 AM. At first he thinks it is nothing to be worried about. Then he begins to think he is going to get laid off, and he gets angry. *How could he lay me off? I have been a faithful employee for years. I am not going to give him the satisfaction. I'm going to see my boss this Wednesday and quit.* But he doesn't, because his wife threatens to leave him if he does something so foolish.

Well, maybe they aren't going to lay me off, he reasons. Now he is double-minded and therefore anxious. By Thursday afternoon, he is convinced they are going to lay him off, and now he is depressed. *How am I going to pay my bills and Melissa's college education?* By Friday morning he is an emotional basket case. He has experienced anger, anxiety, and depression because of the way he has mentally processed the information he had. However, none of his feelings conformed to reality, because his boss had arranged for him to be honored with a promotion and a raise!

The Outcome of Wrong Sexual Thoughts

Our society seems to be ignorant of what sexual and violent impressions can do to our minds, as illustrated by the concept of "adults only." The phrase implies there are separate standards of morality for adults than there are for children. Television programs announce, "The following content is suitable for 'mature' audiences only. Viewer discretion is advised." The content isn't suitable for anyone, and mature people should be the first to know that. Adults should be mature enough to not allow their minds to be programmed with filth. In regard to evil, we should all be like infants: restricting ourselves to only wholesome entertainment. We have already been advised by God concerning sexual immorality in any form: "Flee" (1 Corinthians 6:18).

Since we have no control over how we feel, let me encourage you to drop the following line from your repertoire, whether you use it in reference to yourself or to others: "You shouldn't feel that way." That's a subtle form of rejection, because we can't change how we feel. I am trying to make the point that our feelings are primarily a product of our thought life. What we believe, how we think, and how we perceive ourselves and the world around us determines how we feel.

Suppose you are paddling a canoe down a beautiful river in the wilderness, enjoying God's creation. As you round a bend in the river, your serenity is disturbed. Standing on the riverbank is someone of the opposite sex. The person appears to be very attractive physically and beckons you toward the shore. There is a blanket spread on the bank, and your mind and emotions suddenly go wild with tempting possibilities. You look around, and there is nobody else present. Your heart races and your palms are moist. *What an enticing opportunity. We're all alone out here. She is beckoning me to come over, and there are no witnesses.* Ignoring your convictions, you paddle toward the shore with your emotions reading 9 on a scale of 1 to 10.

But as you draw nearer the shore, you see distress instead of seduction in the woman's face, and you notice small sores. She may be suffering from AIDS. You suddenly realize your initial impression of the stranger was all wrong, and your emotions change from sexual arousal to revulsion. Even that is a flesh response. The Holy Spirit would likely move you to compassion for a person in need. You had a totally wrong perception, but your feelings responded to what you wanted to believe. It's clear the person wasn't beckoning you to the shore for a romantic interlude, but was calling for help after getting into trouble because of illness. You confess to God your wrong thoughts and desires, and then you assist the person.

Your initial thoughts about the woman were wrong, therefore what you felt was a distortion of reality. If what we see or mentally visualize is morally wrong, then our emotions are going to be bound to the wrong stimulus. That is why true romantic Christian love is associated with love and trust, but sexual immorality is often tied into fear and danger. It is actually *eros,* or erotic love, rather than *agape* love. If you want to feel right, you must think right.

The same mental process happens if you see a high-priced call girl who is dressed seductively. At first you are attracted—but would you be if you saw her the way God sees her? What if you could see the condition of her soul? Would it be a pretty sight? Mature Christians look beyond the external, but it would take a very mature Christian to totally ignore the seduction and see a person who is created in the image of God who needs the Lord. Those who are still struggling with lust could have no such ministry.

Check for Viruses

Reprogramming our minds is the path to maturity, but we had better check for viruses. It is important to know that all computer viruses are intentional. Paul writes, "The Spirit clearly says that in later times some will abandon the faith and follow deceiving spirits and things taught by demons" (1 Timothy 4:1). I have counseled hundreds of people who struggle with their thoughts, and some who literally hear "voices." In most cases, the root problem has proven to be a spiritual battle for their minds.

If Satan can get us to believe a lie, he will gain some measure of control over our feelings and behavior. He is intent on destroying a proper perception of God, of ourselves, of members of the opposite sex—including our spouses—and the world we live in. Our problems don't just stem from what we have believed in the past. Paul says we are to presently and continuously take every thought captive and make it obedient to Christ (see 2 Corinthians 10:5).

Unforgiveness

The word "thought" in the above verse is the Greek word *noema*, which only occurs about six times in Scripture, five of which are in 2 Corinthians. Notice the context and topic Paul is addressing when he uses this word, *noema*, elsewhere in 2 Corinthians. "If you forgive anyone, I also forgive him. And what I have forgiven—if there was anything to forgive—I have forgiven in the sight of Christ for your sake, in order that Satan might not outwit us. For we are not unaware of his schemes *[noema]*" (2:10-11).

Nothing will keep us in bondage to our past more than unforgiveness, and it displeases God. God Himself will turn us over to the "torturers" if we don't forgive others from our hearts (Matthew 18:34 NASB), because He doesn't want us chained to the past. *Torturers* is the same word that the demons used when they asked Jesus why He was tormenting them. I believe the greatest access Satan has to the church is our unwillingness to forgive those who have offended us. This has certainly been true of the thousands of people I have been privileged to work with.

If you have been sexually abused, you have probably struggled with thoughts like *I can't forgive that person*, or *I hate that person*, or *I don't want to forgive him, I want him or her to suffer as much as I suffered*. Satan is probably tormenting you. But you say, "You don't know how bad that person hurt me." Such words reveal that they are still hurting you.

Forgiveness is the means by which we set ourselves free from abusers. We are to forgive as Christ has forgiven us. He did that by taking upon Himself the consequences for our sins. When we choose to forgive others, we are agreeing to live with the consequences of their sins. You may be thinking, *That's not fair!* True, but you will have to live with the consequences anyway. The only real choice is whether you do it in the bondage of bitterness or the freedom of forgiveness. "Then where is the justice?" you ask. It is in the cross. Jesus died once for all our sins. "But why should I let the abuser off my hook?" That is why you forgive, so that you are no longer hooked to them. They are not off God's hook, though. Revenge is His, and there will be a final judgment.

Lies from Satan

Consider another passage in 2 Corinthians: "The god of this age [Satan] has blinded the minds *[noema]* of unbelievers, so that they cannot see the light of the gospel of the glory of Christ" (4:4). The one who raises up thoughts against the knowledge of God has a field day with the sexually abused. "Where is your God now?" he taunts. "If God is love, why does He allow the innocent to suffer? If God is all-powerful, why didn't He stop that person from violating you?" The lies of Satan have blinded many people to the truth.

Let's look at one more verse: "I am afraid that just as Eve was deceived by the serpent's cunning, your minds *[noema]* may somehow be led astray from your sincere and pure devotion to Christ" (2 Corinthians 11:3). I'm concerned too, because I see so many people living in bondage to the serpent's lies, which draw them away from their devotion to Christ.

Satan is the father of lies, and he will work on our minds to destroy our concept of God and our understanding of who we are as children of God. People in bondage seldom know who they are in Christ. That is the one common denominator in every person I have been privileged to help find freedom in Christ. Satan can't do anything about our position in Christ, but if he can get us to believe it isn't true, we will live as though it isn't.

Satan's Targets

Satan preys on the minds of wounded people—the victims of broken marriages, the children of alcoholics, those who were sexually abused. They are prime candidates for Satan's lies because their minds have already been pummeled by self-doubt, fear, anger, and hatred because of their abuse. But you don't have to be the victim of a broken home or a painful childhood to be the target of the enemy's temptations, accusations, and deceptions.

For example, suppose in a vulnerable moment a young woman has a tempting sexual thought toward another woman. At first she can't believe she could be tempted to homosexuality. She is embarrassed and immediately flees from the tempting situation. But she decides not to tell anyone about it. Who would understand? Then when it happens again and again, she begins to wonder, *Why am I thinking like this? Is there something wrong with me? Could I be one of them?* Now that the door of doubt is open, she begins to seriously question her sexuality.

If her mind continues to dwell on those tempting thoughts, it will affect the way she feels. That's the way God made us. If she believes what she feels and behaves accordingly, she will use her body as an instrument of unrighteousness and sin will reign in her mortal body. To resolve this, she must renounce that sexual use of her body with any other person, renounce the lie that she is homosexual, and renew her mind with the truth of God's Word.

Don't assume that all disturbing thoughts are from Satan. We live in a sinful world with tempting images and messages all around us. You have memories of hurtful experiences, which prompt thoughts contrary to the knowledge of God. Whether a thought is introduced into your mind from the television set, your memory bank, the pit of hell, or your own imagination doesn't matter in one sense, because we are instructed to take *every* thought captive in obedience to Christ. If it isn't true, don't think it or believe it.

THE POWER OF CHOOSING TRUTH

While I was speaking at a camp, a mother called and asked if she and her 12-year-old son could spend an hour with me. The husband couldn't come, though he wanted to. This was a very close family of three. The young boy was a leader at school and church, but one Sunday he had been overwhelmed by homosexual thoughts toward the pastor. The boy had such a good relationship with his parents that he told them about it. That was highly unusual, and it was just as unusual that the parents knew what to do about it. They recognized where those thoughts were coming from. They instructed their son not to pay any attention to them and to keep choosing the truth, which he did. By the time we met, the thoughts were completely gone. Had he not told his parents, he probably would have thought something was terribly wrong with him, and eventually acted on his impulses—and the whole family would have been torn up.

As I have shared the above story around the country, many people have talked with me afterward and shared that this is exactly what happened to them. They struggled with tempting thoughts and failed to take those thoughts captive to the obedience of Christ. They wondered why they were thinking such thoughts and came to the wrong conclusion that they must be gay. What if those thoughts weren't their thoughts and they had known it? The outcome would have been totally different.

You can try to analyze the source of every thought, but it won't resolve the problem. Too much of the recovery movement is caught up in the paralysis of analysis—and even a perfect analysis of the problem doesn't bring relief. The answer is a personal relationship with Christ. His truth will set us free if we believe it. We will experience this freedom and His presence if we repent.

Cleaning Up the Mind by Choosing the Truth

If you deal with tempting thoughts by trying to rebuke every negative thought, it won't work. You will be like the person in the middle of a lake treading water and trying to keep a dozen corks submerged. You knock one down, another comes up. Instead, you should ignore the stupid corks and swim to shore. As believers, we are not called to dispel the darkness, we are called to turn on the light. We overcome negative thoughts by choosing the truth, as Paul instructs:

> Do not be anxious about anything, but in everything, by prayer and petition, with thanksgiving, present your requests to God. And the peace of God which transcends all understanding, will guard your hearts and your minds [*noema*] in Christ Jesus.

> Finally, brothers, whatever is true, whatever is noble, whatever is right, whatever is pure, whatever is lovely, whatever is admirable—if anything is excellent or praiseworthy—think about such things.

> Whatever you have learned or received or heard from me, or seen in me—put it into practice. And the God of peace will be with you (Philippians 4:6-9).

The Greek word for *anxiety* comes from two root words, which mean "divide" and "mind." The anxious person is double-minded, which will always be true for those struggling with lust and sexual addictions. The first thing we do is turn to God in prayer when we find ourselves in such a state. But that alone is not enough. Next we must assume our responsibility to think about that which is true, noble, and so on. But even that is not enough. We *do* the true, noble, right, pure, and lovely thing. Then the peace of God will be with us.

Those who only hear the word and don't do it are deluded, according to James 1:22. We can do these things if we have genuinely repented by submitting to God and resisting the devil. Those who are experiencing their freedom in Christ can process new truth and grow in Him. Those who haven't fully repented are bopping down corks. They are barely surviving as they tread water in the cesspool of life.

Paul wanted to give the church at Corinth solid food, but he couldn't because they were not able to receive it (1 Corinthians 3:2). So he had to give them only milk. They weren't able to receive it, because of the jealousy and strife among them (verse 3). If there were no way to resolve the personal problems people are having, then there would be no way for them to grow. The good news is, we can resolve our personal and spiritual conflicts through genuine repentance and faith in God.

When I was a young Christian, I decided to clean up my mind. I had a relatively good upbringing, for which I am thankful, but I didn't become a Christian until my mid-twenties. After four years in the Navy, my mind was polluted with a lot of junk. I had seen enough pornography aboard ship to plague me for years. Images would dance in my mind for months after one look. I hated it. I struggled every time I went to a place where pornography was available.

When I made the decision to clean up my mind, do you think the battle got easier or harder? It got harder, of course. Temptation isn't much of a battle if you easily give in to it. It is fierce when you decide to stand against it. I finally got the victory, however. The following illustration may be helpful as you set out to rid your mind of years of impure thoughts.

Think of your polluted mind as a pot filled to the brim with stale black coffee. It is dark and smelly. There is no way to get the pollution of coffee out of the liquid. However, sitting beside the coffeepot is a huge bowl of crystal-clear ice, which represents the Word of God. Your goal is to purify the contents of the pot by adding ice cubes to it every day. I wish there were a way to dump all the cubes (words of the Bible) in at one time, but there isn't. Every cube dilutes the mixture, though, making it a little purer. You can only put in one or two cubes a day, so the process seems almost futile at first. But over the course of time, the water begins to look less and less polluted, and the taste and smell of coffee decreases. The process continues to work, provided you don't add more coffee grounds. If you read your Bible and then look at pornography, you are treading water at best.

Paul writes, "Let the peace of Christ rule in your hearts, since as members of one body you were called to peace. And be thankful" (Colossians 3:15). How do we rid ourselves of evil thoughts, purify our mind, and allow the peace of Christ to reign? The answer is found in the next verse (3:16): "Let the word of Christ dwell in you richly."

The psalmist gives similar instruction:

> How can a young man keep his way pure? By living according to your word. I seek you with all my heart; do not let me stray from your commands. I have hidden your word in my heart that I might not sin against you (Psalm 119:9-11).

Merely trying to stop thinking bad thoughts won't work. We must fill our minds with the pure, clear Word of God. There is no alternative plan. We overcome the father of lies by choosing the truth!

A Winnable Battle

You may find that winning the battle for your mind will initially be two steps forward and one step back. Gradually it will become three steps forward and one step back, then four and five steps forward as you learn to take every thought captive and make it obedient to Christ. You may despair with all your steps backward, but God won't give up on you. Remember, your sins are already forgiven. This is a winnable battle because you are alive in Christ and dead to sin. The bigger war has already been won by Christ.

Freedom to be all that God has called you to be is the greatest blessing in this present life. This freedom is worth fighting for. As you learn more about who you are as a child of God and about the nature of the battle waging for your mind, the process becomes easier. Eventually it is twenty steps forward and one back, and finally the steps are all forward, with only an occasional slip in the battle for the mind.

QUESTIONS FOR DISCUSSION AND THOUGHT

1. How has previous programming of your mind before you came to Christ made it difficult for you to accept the truth recorded in God's Word about yourself, your heavenly Father, and the world we live in?

2. Since your mind was "programmed" to think and believe a certain way before you came to Christ, how did the program change the moment you came to Christ?

3. What happens if we don't take thoughts captive to the obedience of Christ?

4. Why do we rationalize our destructive thoughts after we make a wrong decision?

5. How does our outer person correlate with our inner person?

6. Is lust a problem of the sex glands? Why or why not?

7. Can you explain this statement: "If what we think does not conform to truth, then what we feel does not reflect reality?"

8. Can you explain the spiritual battle for our minds?

9. What could potentially happen if we pay attention to deceiving spirits and believe their lies?

10. How can we renew our minds?

RECOVERY
IN CHRIST

*When I nominated Jesus as my supreme ecologist, years
of inner pollution became instantly biodegradable.*

DONALD R. BROWN

Nancy, a devoted wife and mother, attended our "Living Free in Christ" conference. During the sessions I related several stories of persons who had experienced abuse and found their freedom in Christ. As Nancy listened to the testimonies she felt nauseated, dizzy, and disgusted. Later in the week she confronted me with stern questions: "Why are you telling these awful stories? Those poor children were not at fault. I'm so angry with you. Why are you doing this?"

I wasn't surprised by Nancy's response, because the conference often brings to light in people a lot of problems that haven't been dealt with. I told her, "These stories are not intended to cause pain—they are stories of victory and hope. I don't think your response has anything to do with me or the testimonies. The Lord is using this conference to bring to the surface something in your life that hasn't been resolved, and the evil one doesn't like it. He's behind your agitation. Please talk with one of our Freedom in Christ staff members, who can arrange a personal appointment for you." For the rest of that morning and part of the afternoon Nancy was led through the Steps to Freedom.

Two weeks later Nancy shared her testimony with me, which related to a bedtime story she had often read to her children, *The Bears on Hemlock Mountain*. She recounted how Jonathan, the main character in the story, trudged up the mountain to fetch a large kettle for his mother. On the way he sang, "There are no bears on Hemlock Mountain. No bears. No bears. No bears at all."

However, he did see dark figures in the distance that looked like bears. But he knew they couldn't be bears, because he didn't want to believe there were bears on Hemlock Mountain. So he continued to climb and sing, "There are no bears on Hemlock Mountain. No bears. No bears. No bears at all." Then he saw a bear. He quickly scrambled under the kettle for safety. He remained hidden until his father and uncles arrived with their guns to rescue him from the bear.

Nancy said that she had been struggling with a "dark figure" from her past, but she had not allowed her mind to accept the possibility that there were bears on her mountain of pain: "There was no sexual molestation in my past, no sexual molestation at all." But there were "bear tracks" everywhere. Memories of sexual abuse flooded her mind, but she didn't want to admit it and face the truth. She had hidden under a kettle of denial until she couldn't hide anymore.

During the conference, she learned that she no longer needed to be afraid, because her heavenly Father had overcome the painful threat of the "bear"—sexual abuse. He had already destroyed the "bear," and facing the truth was her only way to get off the mountain of despair. After she had renounced the unrighteous use of her body and forgiven her abuser, there was peace in her life and safety at last on "Hemlock Mountain."

⋄⋅⟝⊜⟞⋅⋄

Perhaps your experience parallels that of Nancy. The truth and testimonies in the previous chapters of this book have brought into sharp focus your shame, failure, and pain in the area of sexual promiscuity, sexual disorientation, or sexual abuse. You may have been in denial for years, insisting, "I don't have a problem." But your lack of peace and victory regarding the sexual sin in your life has worn you down. Try as you might to avoid it, you keep falling into the same thoughts and behaviors again and again. You're too tired to run away anymore. You're ready to throw off the chains of sexual bondage, as made possible by Christ.

I have shared throughout this book that establishing your freedom in Christ comes through knowing and believing the truth, followed by genuine repentance. In the next final chapter of this book you will be given the opportunity to process the Steps to Freedom in Christ. This is a repentance process of submitting to God and resisting the devil (James 4:7).*

Take the Initiative

A prerequisite to establishing your freedom from sexual bondage is to face the truth, acknowledge the problem, and assume responsibility to change. You are responsible for your own confession and repentance of sin. No one can do that for you. Inherent in this process is your willingness to submit to God completely without trying to hide anything from Him. Adam and Eve were created to live in a transparent relationship with God. They walked with God daily in the Garden, naked and unashamed. When they sinned, Adam and Eve covered their nakedness and tried to avoid God.

It is foolish to try hiding from an all-knowing God. We mistakenly think that if we go about our daily business, God won't see us hiding in the darkness. We must give up our defensive, self-protective posture and walk in the light of His presence.

Repentance means to have a change of mind. It is far more than just mental acknowledgment, however. It means to turn from our self-centered and self-indulging ways and trust in God. It means to no longer hold iniquity in our hearts. Repentance involves not only what we turn *from* but who we turn *to*. Those who turn to God are responding to the invitation given by Jesus:

> Come to me, all you who are weary and burdened, and I will give you rest. Take my yoke upon you and learn from me,

---

* These Steps were first introduced in 1990 in *The Bondage Breaker* (Harvest House, 2nd edition, 2000). The theology and methodology are further explained in my book *Discipleship Counseling* (Regal Books, 2003).

for I am gentle and humble in heart, and you will find rest
for your souls. For my yoke is easy and my burden is light
(Matthew 11:28-29).

When we come to Jesus, we should become faithful stewards
of everything God has entrusted to us (1 Corinthians 4:1-2). That
includes our possessions, our ministries, our families, our minds, and
our physical bodies. Repentance means that we renounce any previous
use of our lives and possessions in the service of sin and then dedicate
ourselves to the Lord. In so doing, we are saying that the god of this
world no longer has any right to us, because we belong to Jesus.

The Issue of Forgiveness

Forgiveness is often the most difficult step for anyone who has suffered severely at the hands of a sexual offender. As difficult as it may
be, forgiving your offender actually sets you free from them and the
offense. You must choose to forgive for your own sake. It is the only
way to be free from your past and begin the healing process. You don't
heal in order to forgive—you forgive in order to heal.

As you process this step in the next chapter, Satan may try to
convince you that forgiving the offender somehow makes what he or
she did right. That's a lie. What the offender did to you can never be
justified. You were stripped of your innocence and used for someone
else's pleasure. That person owes you a debt that can never be paid.
The wrongs of the past do not become right when you forgive, but by
forgiving you can be free of them.

In forgiving, you must relinquish your anger, which may have
been used as a defense against other violations. Your anger is both a
signal that you have been threatened or hurt, and also a motivation
to take action. The proper action to take is to forgive and then set up
scriptural boundaries so the offender cannot hurt you again. When
you deal with the offense, the anger will dissipate. When you choose
to forgive by facing all your painful memories—the hate, the hurt,
the ugliness of what the offender did to you—you will be free. Step 3
in chapter 9 will guide you through this important process.

Beth had been sexually abused. Her behavior was tearing up her parents and destroying their Christian home. Usually nothing good comes from appointments made by parents for children who don't want to be helped, but Beth's parents assured me she wanted to see me.

Her opening statement was, "I don't want to get right with God or anything like that!" I have learned that such statements are just a dodge, and I don't let them discourage me. I said, "I am willing to accept your choices. But since you're here, maybe you could share with me how you have been hurt." She told me the story of being date-raped by the campus athletic "hero" at her high school. At the time she was too embarrassed to tell anyone about it, and she had no idea how to resolve it. Having lost her virginity, she became sexually promiscuous, living off and on with an immoral man.

I asked Beth's permission to lead her through the Steps, and she agreed. When I invited her to ask the Lord to reveal to her mind every sexual use of her body as an instrument of unrighteousness, she said, "That would be embarrassing!" So I stepped out of the room while a female prayer partner helped her through the process. That night she was singing in church for the first time in years. She was experiencing her freedom.

A New Beginning

The Steps to Freedom in Christ are not an end in themselves. They offer a new beginning. For some people, successfully processing the Steps will be the first major victory in an ongoing battle. The following testimony is from a man who was formerly trapped in nearly every form of sexual bondage mentioned in this book. It illustrates the process of securing freedom in Christ one victory at a time.

> My dad left our home when I was four years old. Every day I cried out to God to bring my daddy home. But he never came back. So my mother, my brother, and I moved in with my grandparents. I disconnected from God early in life because no one tried to explain why He never answered my pleas.

One night my grandfather undressed in front of me and my grandmother. He had an erection. Although he wouldn't have done anything to hurt me, my grandfather's act of indiscretion left a terrible mark in my mind that surfaced years later.

In the absence of my father, as a young boy I bonded with my grandfather. I thought he loved me. It didn't matter to me that he had been unfaithful to my grandmother, had sexually abused my mother, and was becoming an alcoholic. When my mother remarried and we moved away, I felt like I had lost my father for a second time. But I didn't bother to ask God for help, because I felt He had let me down.

We moved every year as I grew up. Every time I made a friend, we moved again, keeping the wounds of abandonment and loneliness painful. I grieved over every loss and did everything to protect myself from being hurt again.

I believed I was different from most boys. I started playing sexually with some of my male friends during grade school. Voices in my head told me it was okay, because I was born that way. I had a terrible male void in my life, and my heart burned with desire. The memory of seeing my grandfather with an erection prompted a fascination with seeing boys and men naked. Voyeurism became a way of life for me.

Meanwhile, my own family was being ripped apart by conflict. The squabbles and fights mortified me. I was a loyal and sensitive kid who carried a deep concern for everyone in my family. I tried to convince my friends' parents to adopt me in order to escape the turmoil, but it didn't work. I finally detached completely from my mother and brother.

As an adolescent and young adult, I threw myself into the gay world. I was addicted to watching men in public restrooms, and I visited gay bars almost every night. When I found a gay lover, I thought I had finally met a man who would love me and stay with me forever. I was emotionally codependent on him. When the relationship ended after three years, I fell into a deep depression. I was emotionally bankrupt and lost. News of my brother's death added to my sense of despair and abandonment.

At his funeral I purchased a Bible, but I didn't know why. I kept it on my nightstand with a cross someone had given me. I didn't dare move them. I was terrified every night, feeling a horrifying dark presence around me. Someone told me to hold the cross and yell, "I bind you in the name of Jesus Christ of Nazareth." I did so night after night with the covers pulled up to my neck. But something kept tormenting me.

I finally started reading the Bible and attending church. I accepted the Lord at a baptism service and left the gay lifestyle completely. I studied the Word seriously, but with my background it was easy to fall into legalism. I didn't understand grace and forgiveness. The Bible talked a lot about sexual immorality and clearly forbade homosexual behavior. I asked myself, *If I am a Christian, why do I still feel the same homosexual tendencies?*

The more I tried to do what the Bible said and what others expected of me, the more guilt I felt. I didn't dare tell anyone what I was feeling. The voyeurism became intense and triggered an uncontrollable bondage to masturbation.

When I began teaching a Sunday school class, the voices in my head condemned me daily and accused me of being a hypocrite. I believed them. I was tormented. The more I fought back by reading my Bible and serving the Lord, the greater the oppression became. My mind was ruled by immoral thoughts. I experienced intense sexual dreams. I was out of control and backsliding quickly. I found myself back in public restrooms. I talked to Christian counselors and pastors, but no one seemed to be able to offer a workable solution to my problem. I wanted so badly to know and serve the Lord.

A friend who was aware of my struggle gave me a copy of *Victory over the Darkness* by Neil Anderson. As I began reading it, the book seemed to be written about me. For the first time I understood how I had gotten into my horrible condition and how I could get out of it. No one had ever told me I was a child of God, that God had chosen me as His friend, and that He loved me specifically. I had learned about God intellectually, but through reading this book I finally met my gentle and loving heavenly Father personally.

When I read *The Bondage Breaker,* I knew I was spiritually oppressed. I had been involved in almost everything in the non-Christian spiritual experience inventory at the end of the book. I began to understand my oppressive thought life, rampant voyeurism, and low sense of worth. I discovered that realizing I am a child of God was the answer to breaking the destructive cycle that had been present in my family for generations.

I learned that Jesus is the Bondage Breaker and that I have authority over the kingdom of darkness because I am seated with Christ in the heavenlies. However, the more I embraced these truths, the more I was attacked. I was falling apart emotionally. I had to see Neil Anderson.

I attended one of his conferences and my entire life was changed. One of his staff met with me in a four-hour session. No one had ever wanted to spend that much time with me. I felt free for the first time in my life. Still, my desperate need for affirmation prevented me from being totally honest in the counseling session.

Two days later Neil talked about forgiving others. I asked him if a person has to cry when they forgive someone. He didn't answer. He made me think about it. On the way back to my motel, I told the Lord I really wanted to forgive my dad and stepdad for not validating me. Then the Lord let me feel the pain of not being validated. He gave me a glimpse of His pain on the cross. I cried so hard I could hardly drive. Then I thought of the women in my life that had hurt me so badly. The floodgates opened as I forgave each person from my heart.

I was free, but Neil shared with me that people who have been in bondage a long time are more like onions than bananas. You peel a banana once, and that's it. But an onion has many layers. He cautioned me that I had successfully worked through at least one layer of my problem. Other layers might surface, but at least I knew how to respond when they did.

After a couple of months, the glow of my freedom subsided. I started to backslide and return to voyeurism. I read several of Neil's books. I fought back against the attack and worked through the issues. Another layer of the onion was peeled away. I felt renewed again, but also worn out from the battle. I wasn't reading the Word or praying much. I didn't feel like doing it.

So I started reading Neil and Joanne's devotional, *Daily in Christ*. I was filled with guilt because of my mental lapses into voyeurism and masturbation. How could I teach Sunday school and be such a hypocrite? I told the Lord I really loved Him and wanted to serve Him. Then I decided to prove it. I had always been fearful of vows, but I made one. I told the Lord I was His child and I was going to be baptized again. I knew that I didn't have to and that baptism didn't save me, but I wanted to erect a milestone for the Lord like the Israelites did when they crossed the Jordan.

I made the vow, and the Lord honored it beyond my wildest anticipation. He confirmed in me that I was a child of God and that He loved me. Once I submitted myself completely to Him and stopped trying to fix myself, He was able to do it for me.

The masturbation stopped instantaneously and has never come back. The voyeurism has also stopped. I have learned what it means to take every thought captive in obedience to Christ. Now I measure everything that comes into my mind against what the Lord says in His Word, and the truth has set me free.

Now that I know I am a child of God, there is no more low self-worth, inferiority, obsessive, negative, or perverse thoughts, or secret behavior. I busted through that last layer of the onion like a rocket. There may be more layers ahead, but this time I am armed with the Lord's belt of truth.

It Is for Your Freedom

You will be tempted to end your reading of this book after this chapter and not finish the course. You may also be tempted to read the next chapter, but not process it. That would be like standing inside a prison near an open door and never leaving, even though the Lord is standing on the outside beckoning you to come. If you are reading this book on your own, then find a safe place and give yourself the best possible opportunity to process the Steps. If you are studying this book with others, then take advantage of the opportunity to go through the Steps as a group. If you and your group processes them as written, there will be no spiritual manifestations, and nobody will be embarrassed by any public disclosures. You will be invited to pray some prayers out loud as a group asking God to guide you, but you will be given the opportunity to respond to God privately on your own.

Your experience of going through the Steps to Freedom in Christ may be different from the experiences of others. Each individual is unique because each person has different issues to resolve. Some people are elated by the overwhelming sense of peace they feel the first time. Others may have that experience as well, but may have to work through many layers first. If you have repressed memories, God will graciously reveal them one layer at a time—probably because we couldn't handle doing it all at once.

Paul wrote, "It is for freedom that Christ has set us free" (Galatians 5:1). Once we have tasted our freedom in Christ, we must maintain our relationship with God by continuing to stand in the truth of His Word. Paul completes the verse by encouraging us to: "Stand firm, then, and do not let yourselves be burdened again by a yoke of slavery." Freedom is our inheritance, but we must not turn our freedom into ritualistic rules and regulations, which is legalism, or an opportunity to indulge our fleshly nature, which is license (Galatians 5:13). The steps you take to experience your freedom in Christ are not the end of the journey but the beginning of a walk by faith in the power of the Holy Spirit. Therefore, let me encourage you to do what Paul wrote in Galatians 5:16,

Walk by the Spirit, and you will not
carry out the desire of the flesh.

QUESTIONS FOR DISCUSSION AND THOUGHT

1. Why are some afraid to acknowledge obvious signs of abuse?

2. Why should we forgive those who have offended or abused us?

3. What insight did you gain from the man's testimony of overcoming homosexuality?

4. What must we do if we want to live a liberated life in Christ?

5. Are you going to do it?

PART TWO

9

THE STEPS TO
FREEDOM IN CHRIST

God created Adam and Eve to be spiritually alive, which means that their souls were in union with God. Living in a dependent relationship with their heavenly Father, they were to exercise dominion over the earth. Acting independently of God, they chose to disobey Him, and their choice to sin separated them from God. Consequently, all their descendants are born physically alive but spiritually dead— that is, separated from God.

Since we have all sinned and fallen short of the glory of God (Romans 3:23), we remain separated from Him and cannot fulfill the original purpose for our creation, which is to glorify God and enjoy His presence forever. Satan became the rebel holder of authority, and the god of this world. Jesus referred to him as the ruler of this world, and the apostle John wrote that the whole world lies in the power of the evil one (1 John 5:19).

The Whole Gospel

Jesus came to undo the works of Satan (1 John 3:8) and take upon Himself the sins of the world. By dying for our sins, Jesus removed the enmity that existed between God and those He created in His image. The resurrection of Christ brought new life to those who put their trust in Him. Every born-again believer's soul is again in union with God, and this is most often communicated in the New Testament as being "in Christ," or "in Him." The apostle Paul explained that anyone who is *in Christ* is a new creation (2 Corinthians 5:17). The apostle John wrote, "As many as received Him, to them He gave the right to become children of God, to those who believe in His name" (John 1:12), and he also wrote, "See how great a love the Father has bestowed on us, that we would be called children of God; and such we are" (1 John 3:1).

No amount of effort on your part can save you, and neither can any religious activity, no matter how well intentioned. We are saved by putting our trust in God, based on the finished work of Christ. "By grace you have been saved through faith; and that not of yourselves, it is the gift of God; not as a result of works, so that no one may boast" (Ephesians 2:8-9). If you have never received Christ, you can do so right now. God knows the thoughts and intentions of your heart, so all you have to do is put your trust in God alone. You can express your decision in prayer as follows:

> *Dear heavenly Father, thank You for sending Jesus to die on the cross for my sins. I acknowledge that I have sinned and that I cannot save myself. I believe that Jesus came to give me life, and by faith I now choose to receive You into my life as my Lord and Savior. May the power of Your indwelling presence enable me to be the person You created me to be. I pray that You would grant me repentance leading to a knowledge of the truth so that I can experience my freedom in Christ and be transformed by the renewing of my mind. In Jesus' precious name I pray. Amen.*

Assurance of Salvation

Paul wrote, "If you confess with your mouth Jesus as Lord, and believe in your heart that God raised Him from the dead, you will be saved" (Romans 10:9). Do you believe that God the Father raised Jesus from the dead? Did you invite Jesus to be your Lord and Savior? Then you are a child of God, and nothing can separate you from the love of Christ (Romans 8:35). Your heavenly Father has sent His Holy Spirit to live within you and testify to your spirit that you are a child of God (Romans 8:16). "You were sealed *in Him* with the Holy Spirit of promise" (Ephesians 1:13). The Holy Spirit will guide you into all truth (John 16:13).

Resolving Personal and Spiritual Conflicts

Since we were all born dead (spiritually) in our trespasses and sin (Ephesians 2:1), we had neither the presence of God in our lives nor the knowledge of His ways. Consequently, we all learned to live our lives independent of God. When we became new creations in Christ, our minds were not instantly renewed. That is why Paul wrote,

> Do not conform any longer to the pattern of this world, but
> be transformed by the renewing of your mind. Then you will
> be able to test and approve what God's will is—His good,
> pleasing, and perfect will (Romans 12:2).

That is why new Christians struggle with many of the same old thoughts and habits. Their minds have been previously programmed to live independently of God. That is the chief characteristic of our old nature, or flesh. As new creations in Christ, we have the mind of Christ, and the Holy Spirit will lead us into all truth.

To experience our freedom in Christ and grow in the grace of God requires repentance, which literally means a "change of mind." Repentance is not something we can do on our own, therefore we need to submit to God and resist the devil (James 4:7). The Steps to Freedom in Christ (the Steps) are designed to help you do that. Submitting to God is the critical issue. He is the Wonderful Counselor and the One who grants repentance leading to a knowledge of the truth (2 Timothy 2:24-26).

The Steps cover seven critical issues between ourselves and God. We will not experience our freedom in Christ if we seek false guidance, believe lies, fail to forgive others as we have been forgiven, live in rebellion, respond in pride, fail to acknowledge our sin, and continue in the sins of our ancestors:

> He who conceals his transgressions will not prosper, but he

who confesses and forsakes [renounces] them will find compassion (Proverbs 28:13).

Since we have this ministry, as we received mercy, we do not lose heart, but we renounced things hidden because of shame, not walking in craftiness or adulterating the word of God, but by the manifestation of truth (2 Corinthians 4:1-2).

Even though Satan is defeated, he still rules this world through a hierarchy of demons who tempt, accuse, and deceive those who fail to put on the armor of God, stand firm in their faith, and take every thought captive to the obedience of Christ. Our sanctuary is our identity and position in Christ, and we have all the protection we need to live a victorious life—but if we fail to assume our responsibility and give ground to Satan, we will suffer the consequences of our sinful choices, attitudes, and actions. The good news is, we can repent and can reclaim all that we have in Christ, and that is what the Steps will enable you to do.

Processing the Steps

If you are working through these Steps alone, it is best to set aside plenty of time and finish them in one session, which may take you two or more hours. Every step is explained so you will have no trouble doing this. I suggest you find a quiet place where you can process the Steps out loud. If you experience some mental interference, just ignore it and continue on. Thoughts like *This isn't going to work,* or *I don't believe this,* or blasphemous, condemning, and accusing thoughts have no power over you unless you believe them. They are just thoughts, and it doesn't make any difference if they originate from you, an external source, or from Satan and his demons. They will be resolved when you have fully repented.

The mind is the control center, and you will not lose control in the process if you don't lose control of your mind. If you are being mentally harassed, just ignore it. Remember, you are a child of God and seated with Christ in the heavenlies. That means you have the authority and power to do His will.

If you are working through the Steps with a group, the leader will start each step by having the participants pray together, out loud, the opening prayer of each step. You will then be given enough time to finish each step on your own. (Each participant should have a pencil or pen.) All the prayers and declarations that are to be prayed and read out loud will be in italics. After the group has been given sufficient time, the leader should ask if anyone needs any more time. If not, then go on to the next step.

Keep in mind that the Steps don't set you free. *Jesus* sets you free, and you will progressively experience that freedom as you respond to Him in faith and repentance. Don't worry about any demonic interference — most people experience very little. It doesn't make any difference if Satan has a little role or a big role in your problem, the critical issue is your relationship with God, and issues affecting the intimacy of that relationship are what you are resolving. This is a ministry of reconciliation. Once those issues are resolved, Satan has no right to remain. Successfully completing this repentance process is not an end—it is a beginning of growth. Unless these issues are resolved, however, the growth process will be stalled and your Christian life will be stagnant.

Processing these Steps can play a major role in your continuing process of discipleship. The purpose is to get you firmly rooted in Christ. It doesn't take long to establish your identity and freedom in Christ, but there is no such thing as instant maturity. Renewing your mind and conforming to the image of God is a lifelong process. May the Lord grace you with His presence as you seek to do His will. Once you have experienced your freedom in Christ, you can help others experience the joy of their salvation.

All participants should begin the Steps with the following prayer and declaration, doing so in unison and out loud:

PRAYER:

Dear heavenly Father, You are present in this room and in my life. You alone are all-knowing, all-powerful, and everywhere-present, and I worship You alone. I declare my dependency upon

You, for apart from You I can do nothing. I choose to believe Your Word, which teaches that all authority in heaven and earth belongs to the resurrected Christ, and being alive in Christ I have the authority to resist the devil as I submit to You. I ask that You fill me with Your Holy Spirit and guide me into all truth. I ask for Your complete protection and guidance as I seek to know You and do Your will. In the wonderful name of Jesus I pray. Amen.

DECLARATION:

In the name and authority of the Lord Jesus Christ, I command Satan and all evil spirits to release their hold on me in order that I can be free to know and choose to do the will of God. As a child of God who is seated with Christ in the heavenly places, I declare that every enemy of the Lord Jesus Christ in my presence be bound. Satan and all his demons cannot inflict any pain or in any way prevent God's will from being done in my life today, because I belong to the Lord Jesus Christ.

Step 1: Counterfeit vs. Real

The first step toward experiencing your freedom in Christ is to renounce (verbally reject) all involvement (past or present) with occult, cult, or false religious teachings or practices. Participation in any group that denies that Jesus Christ is Lord or elevates any teaching or book to the level of (or above) the Bible must be renounced. In addition, groups that require dark, secret initiations, ceremonies, vows, pacts, or covenants need to be renounced. God does not take lightly false guidance. "As for the person who turns to mediums and to spiritists...I will also set My face against that person and will cut him off from among my people" (Leviticus 20:6). Since you don't want the Lord to cut you off, ask Him to guide you as follows:

Dear heavenly Father, please bring to my mind anything and everything that I have done knowingly or unknowingly that involves occult, cult, or false religious teachings or practices. I want to experience Your freedom by renouncing any and all false guidance. In Jesus' name I pray. Amen.

The Lord may bring things to your mind that you had forgotten, even things you participated in as a game or thought were jokes. You might even have been passively yet curiously watching others participate in counterfeit religious practices. The purpose is to renounce all counterfeit spiritual experiences and their beliefs.

To help bring these things to your mind, prayerfully consider the following Non-Christian Spiritual Checklist. Then pray the prayer following the checklist to renounce each activity or group the Lord brings to mind. He may reveal to you ones that are not on the list. Be especially aware of your need to renounce non-Christian folk religious practices if you have grown up in another culture. It is important that you prayerfully renounce them out loud.

NON CHRISTIAN SPIRITUAL CHECKLIST:

(Check all those that you have participated in.)

- ☐ Out-of-body experience
- ☐ Hypnosis
- ☐ Silva Mind Control
- ☐ Ouija board
- ☐ Astral projection
- ☐ Transcendental meditation
- ☐ Bloody Mary
- ☐ Séances
- ☐ Spirit guides/channelers
- ☐ Occult games
- ☐ Black or white magic
- ☐ Yoga religion

- ☐ Magic Eight Ball
- ☐ Blood pacts
- ☐ Hare Krishna
- ☐ Spells and curses
- ☐ Fetishism/crystals/charms
- ☐ Bahaism
- ☐ Mental telepathy/control
- ☐ Sexual spirits
- ☐ Indian (Native American) spiritism
- ☐ Automatic writing
- ☐ Martial arts (divine masters)
- ☐ Islam
- ☐ Trances
- ☐ Superstitions
- ☐ Hinduism
- ☐ Mormonism
- ☐ Buddhism
- ☐ Fortune telling/divination
- ☐ Jehovah's Witness
- ☐ Rosicrucianism
- ☐ Tarot cards
- ☐ New Age teaching
- ☐ Taoism
- ☐ Levitation
- ☐ Masons
- ☐ False gods (money, sex, power, pleasure, people)
- ☐ Witchcraft/Wicca/sorcery

- ☐ Christian Science
- ☐ Satanism
- ☐ Unification Church (Moonies)
- ☐ Other non-Christian religions (cults, dark movies, video games, fantasy games, and so on)
- ☐ Palm reading
- ☐ The Forum (EST)
- ☐ Astrology/horoscopes
- ☐ Scientology
- ☐ Unitarianism

Additional questions to help you become aware of counterfeit religious experiences:

- ☐ Do you now have, or have you ever had, an imaginary friend, spirit guide, or "angel" offering you guidance or companionship? (If it has a name, renounce it by name).

- ☐ Have you ever heard voices in your head, or had repeating, nagging thoughts such as "I'm dumb," "I'm ugly," "Nobody loves me," "I can't do anything right"—as if there were a conversation going on inside your head?

- ☐ Have you ever been hypnotized, attended a New Age seminar, or consulted a medium or spiritist?

- ☐ Have you ever made a secret vow or pact (or inner vow—that is, "I will never...")?

- ☐ Have you ever been involved in a satanic ritual or attended a concert in which Satan was the focus?

Once you have completed your checklist and the questions, confess and renounce every false religious practice, belief, ceremony, vow, or pact that you were involved in by praying the following prayer aloud if by yourself or silently in a group:

Lord Jesus, I confess that I have participated in (specifically name
every belief and involvement with all that you have checked
above) and I renounce them all as counterfeits. I pray that You
will fill me with Your Holy Spirit that I may be guided by You.
Thank You that in Christ I am forgiven. Amen.

Step 2: Deception vs. Truth

The Christian life is lived by faith according to what God says is true. Jesus is the truth, the Holy Spirit is the Spirit of truth, God's Word is truth, and we are to speak the truth in love (see John 14:6; 16:13; 17:17; Ephesians 4:15). The biblical response to truth is *faith,* regardless of whether we *feel* it is true or not. In addition, Christians are to have no part in lying, deceiving, stretching the truth, or anything else associated with falsehood. Lies keep us in bondage, but it is the truth that sets us free (John 8:32). David wrote, "How blessed [happy] is the man...in whose spirit there is no deceit." Joy and freedom come from walking in the truth.

We find the strength to walk in the light of honesty and transparency before God and others (see 1 John 1:7) when we know that God loves and accepts us just as we are. We can face reality, acknowledge our sins, and not try to hide. Begin this commitment to truth by praying the following prayer out loud. Don't let any opposing thoughts such as *This is a waste of time* or *I wish I could believe this, but I can't,* keep you from pressing forward. God will strengthen you as you rely on Him.

Dear heavenly Father, You are the truth, and I desire to live
by faith according to Your truth. The truth will set me free,
but in many ways I have been deceived by the father of lies, the
philosophies of this fallen world, and I have deceived myself. I
choose to walk in the light, knowing that You love and accept me
just as I am. As I consider areas of possible deception, I invite the
Spirit of truth to guide me into all truth. Please protect me from
all deception as You "search me, O God, and know my heart;
try me and know my anxious thoughts; and see if there be any

hurtful way in me, and lead me in the everlasting way." In the name of Jesus I pray. Amen.

(See Psalm 139:23-24.)

Prayerfully consider the lists in the three exercises below, using the prayers at the end of each exercise in order to confess any ways you have given in to deception or wrongly defended yourself (out loud if alone, privately if in a group). You cannot instantly renew your mind, but the process will never get started without acknowledging your mental strongholds or defense mechanisms, which are sometimes called flesh patterns.

Ways You Can Be Deceived by the World

- ☐ Believing that acquiring money and things will bring lasting happiness (Matthew 13:22; 1 Timothy 6:10)

- ☐ Believing that excessive food and alcohol can relieve my stress and make me happy (Proverbs 23:19-21)

- ☐ Believing that an attractive body and personality will get me what I need (Proverbs 31:10; 1 Peter 3:3-4)

- ☐ Believing that gratifying sexual lust will bring lasting satisfaction (Ephesians 4:22; 1 Peter 2:11)

- ☐ Believing I can sin and get away without any negative consequences (Hebrews 3:12-13)

- ☐ Believing I need more than what God has given me in Christ (2 Corinthians 11:2-4,13-15)

- ☐ Believing I can do whatever I want and no one can touch me (Proverbs 16:18; Obadiah 3; 1 Peter 5:5)

- ☐ Believing that unrighteous people who refuse to accept Christ go to heaven anyway (1 Corinthians 6:9-11)

- ☐ Believing I can associate with bad company and not become corrupted (1 Corinthians 15:33-34)

☐ Believing I can read, see, or listen to anything and not be corrupted (Proverbs 4:23-27; Matthew 5:28)

☐ Believing there are no consequences on earth for my sin (Galatians 6:7-8)

☐ Believing I must gain the approval of certain people in order to be happy (Galatians 1:10)

☐ Believing I must measure up to certain standards in order to feel good about myself (Galatians 3:2-3; 5:1)

Lord Jesus, I confess I have been deceived by (confess the items you checked above). I thank You for Your forgiveness, and I commit myself to believe only Your truth. In Jesus' name I pray. Amen.

Ways to Deceive Yourself

☐ Hearing God's Word but not doing what it says (James 1:22)

☐ Saying I have no sin (1 John 1:8)

☐ Thinking I am something I'm really not (Galatians 6:3)

☐ Thinking I am wise in this worldly age (1 Corinthians 3:18,19)

☐ Thinking I can be truly religious but not bridle my tongue (James 1:26)

☐ Thinking that God is the source of my problems (Lamentations 3)

☐ Thinking I can live my life without the help of anyone else (1 Corinthians 12:14-20)

Lord Jesus, I confess I have deceived myself by (confess the items checked above). Thank You for Your forgiveness. I commit myself to believe only Your truth. In Jesus' name I pray. Amen.

Ways to Wrongly Defend Yourself

- ☐ Denial of reality (conscious or unconscious)
- ☐ Fantasy (escaping reality by daydreaming, TV, movies, music, computer or video games, drugs, alcohol)
- ☐ Emotional insulation (withdrawing from people or keeping people at a distance to avoid rejection)
- ☐ Regression (reverting to less threatening times)
- ☐ Displaced anger (taking out frustrations on innocent people)
- ☐ Projection (attributing to another what you find unacceptable in yourself)
- ☐ Rationalization (making excuses for my own poor behavior)
- ☐ Lying (protecting self through falsehoods)
- ☐ Blaming myself (when not responsible) and others
- ☐ Hypocrisy (presenting a false image)

Lord Jesus, I confess that I have wrongly defended myself by (confess the items checked above). Thank You for Your forgiveness. I trust You to defend and protect me. In Jesus' name I pray. Amen.

The wrong ways we have employed to shield ourselves from pain and rejection are often deeply ingrained in our lives. You may need additional discipling or counseling to learn how to allow Christ to be your rock, fortress, deliverer, and refuge (see Psalm 18:1-2). The more you learn how loving, powerful, and protective God is, the more you'll be likely to trust Him. The more you realize His complete acceptance of you in Christ, the more you'll be released to be open, honest, and (in a healthy way) vulnerable before God and others.

Faith Must Be Based on the Truth of God's Word

The New Age movement has twisted the concept of faith by teaching that we make something true by believing it. That is false. We cannot create reality with our minds; only God can do that. Our responsibility is to *face* reality and choose to believe what God says is true. True biblical faith, therefore, is choosing to believe and act upon what is true, because God has said it is true, and He is the Truth. Faith is something you decide to do, not something you feel like doing. Believing something doesn't make it true—*it's already true, therefore we choose to believe it!* Truth is not conditioned by whether we choose to believe it or not.

Everybody lives by faith. The only difference between Christian faith and non-Christian faith is the object of our faith. If the object of our faith is not trustworthy, then no amount of believing will change that. That's why our faith must be grounded on the solid rock of God's perfect, unchanging character and the truth of His word. For 2000 years Christians have known the importance of verbally and publicly declaring truth. Read aloud and in unison the following Statements of Truth, and carefully consider what you are professing. You may find it helpful to read them aloud daily for several weeks, which will help renew your mind to the truth.

Statements of Truth

1. *I recognize that there is only one true and living God who exists as the Father, Son, and Holy Spirit. He is worthy of all honor, praise, and glory as the One who made all things and holds all things together.* (See Exodus 20:2-3; Colossians 1:16-17.)

2. *I recognize that Jesus Christ is the Messiah, the Word who became flesh and dwelt among us. I believe that He came to destroy the works of the devil, and that He disarmed the rulers and authorities and made a public display of them, having triumphed over them.* (See John 1:1,14; Colossians 2:15; 1 John 3:8.)

3. *I believe that God demonstrated His own love for me in that while I was still a sinner, Christ died for me. I believe that He has delivered me from the domain of darkness and transferred me to His kingdom, and in Him I have redemption, the forgiveness of sins.* (See Romans 5:8; Colossians 1:13-14.)

4. *I believe that I am now a child of God and that I am seated with Christ in the heavenlies. I believe that I was saved by the grace of God through faith, and that it was a gift and not a result of any works on my part.* (See Ephesians 2:6,8-9; 1 John 3:1-3.)

5. *I choose to be strong in the Lord and in the strength of His might. I put no confidence in the flesh, for the weapons of warfare are not of the flesh but are divinely powerful for the destruction of strongholds. I put on the full armor of God. I resolve to stand firm in my faith and resist the evil one.* (See 2 Corinthians 10:4; Ephesians 6:10-20; Philippians 3:3.)

6. *I believe that apart from Christ I can do nothing, so I declare my complete dependence on Him. I choose to abide in Christ in order to bear much fruit and glorify my Father. I announce to Satan that Jesus is my Lord. I reject any and all counterfeit gifts or works of Satan in my life.* (See John 15:5,8; 1 Corinthians 12:3.)

7. *I believe that the truth will set me free and that Jesus is the truth. If He sets me free, I will be free indeed. I recognize that walking in the light is the only path of true fellowship with God and man. Therefore, I stand against all of Satan's deception by taking every thought captive in obedience to Christ. I declare that the Bible is the only authoritative standard for truth and life.* (See John 8:32,36; 14:6; 2 Corinthians 10:5; 2 Timothy 3:15-17; 1 John 1:3-7.)

8. *I choose to present my body to God as a living and holy*

sacrifice and the members of my body as instruments of righ-
teousness. I choose to renew my mind by the living Word of
God in order that I may prove that the will of God is good,
acceptable, and perfect. I put off the old self with its evil
practices and put on the new self. I declare myself to be a new
creation in Christ. (See Romans 6:13; 12:1-2; 2 Corinthians 5:17; Colossians 3:9-10.)

9. *By faith, I choose to be filled with the Spirit so that I can be*
   guided into all truth. I choose to walk by the Spirit so that I
   will not carry out the desires of the flesh. (See John 16:13;
   Galatians 5:16; Ephesians 5:18.)

10. *I renounce all selfish goals and choose the ultimate goal of*
    love. I choose to obey the two greatest commandments: to
    love the Lord my God with all my heart, soul, mind, and
    strength and to love my neighbor as myself. (See Matthew
    22:37-39; 1 Timothy 1:5.)

11. *I believe that the Lord Jesus has all authority in heaven and*
    on earth, and He is the head over all rule and authority. I
    am complete in Him. I believe that Satan and his demons
    are subject to me in Christ since I am a member of Christ's
    body. Therefore, I obey the command to submit to God and
    resist the devil, and I command Satan in the name of Jesus
    Christ to leave my presence. (See Matthew 28:18; Ephe-
    sians 1:19-23; Colossians 2:10; James 4:7.)

Step 3: Bitterness vs. Forgiveness

We are called to be merciful just as our heavenly Father is merciful
(Luke 6:36) and forgive others as we have been forgiven (Ephesians
4:31-32). Doing so sets us free from our past and doesn't allow Satan
to take advantage of us (2 Corinthians 2:10-11). Ask God to bring to
your mind the people you need to forgive by praying the following
prayer aloud:

Dear heavenly Father, I thank You for the riches of Your kindness, forbearance, and patience toward me, knowing that Your kindness has led me to repentance. I confess I have not shown that same kindness and patience toward those who have hurt or offended me. Instead, I have held on to my anger, bitterness, and resentment toward them. Please bring to my mind all the people I need to forgive in order that I may now do so. In Jesus' name I pray. Amen.

(See Romans 2:4.)

On a separate sheet of paper, list the names of people who come to your mind. At this point, don't question whether you need to forgive them or not. Often we hold things against ourselves as well, punishing ourselves for wrong choices we've made in the past. Write "myself" at the bottom of your list if you need to forgive yourself. Forgiving yourself is accepting the truth that God has already forgiven you in Christ. If God forgives you, you can forgive yourself!

Also write down "thoughts against God" at the bottom of your list. Obviously, God has never done anything wrong so He doesn't need our forgiveness, but we need to let go of our disappointments with our heavenly Father. People often harbor angry thoughts against Him because He did not do what they wanted Him to do. Those feelings of anger or resentment toward God need to be released.

Before you begin working through the process of forgiving those on your list, review what forgiveness is and what it is not. The critical points are highlighted in bold print.

Forgiveness Is Not Forgetting

People who want to forget all that was done to them will find they cannot do it. When God says that He will remember our sins no more, He is saying that He will not use the past against us. Forgetting is a long term by-product of forgiveness, but it is never a means toward it. Don't put off forgiving those who have hurt you, hoping the pain will go away. Once you choose to forgive someone, *then* Christ will heal your wounds. We don't heal in order to forgive; we forgive in order to heal.

Forgiveness Is a Choice, a Decision of the Will

Since God requires you to forgive, it is something you can do. Some people hold on to their anger as a means of protecting themselves against further abuse, but all they are doing is hurting themselves. Others want revenge. The Bible teaches, "'Revenge is mine, I will repay,' says the Lord" (Romans 12:19). Let God deal with the person. Let him or her off your hook because as long as you refuse to forgive someone, you are still hooked to that person. You are still chained to your past, bound up in your bitterness. By forgiving, you let the other person off your hook—but he or she is not off God's hook. You must trust that God will deal with the person justly and fairly, something you simply cannot do.

"But you don't know how much this person hurt me!" you might say. No other human really knows another person's pain, but Jesus does, and He instructs us to forgive others for our sake. Until you let go of your bitterness and hate, the person is still hurting you. Nobody can fix your past, but you can be free from it. What you gain by forgiving is freedom from your past and those who have abused you. Forgiveness is to set a captive free and then realize you we were the captive.

Forgiveness Is Agreeing to Live with the Consequences of Another Person's Sin

We are all living with the consequences of someone else's sin. The only choice is to do so in the *bondage of bitterness* or in the *freedom of forgiveness.* But where is the justice? The cross makes forgiveness legally and morally right. Jesus died once for all our sins. We are to forgive as Christ has forgiven us. He did that by taking upon Himself the consequences of our sins. God "made Him who knew no sin to be sin on our behalf, that we might become the righteousness of God in Him" (2 Corinthians 5:21).

Do not wait for the other person to ask for your forgiveness.

Remember, Jesus did not wait for those who were crucifying Him to apologize before He forgave them. Even while they mocked and jeered at Him, He prayed, "Father, forgive them; for they do not know what they are doing" (Luke 23:34).

Forgive from Your Heart

Allow God to bring to the surface the painful memories, and acknowledge how you feel toward those who've hurt you. If your forgiveness doesn't touch the emotional core of your life, it will be incomplete. Too often we're afraid of the pain so we bury our emotions deep down inside us. Let God bring them to the surface so He can begin to heal those damaged emotions.

Forgiveness Is Choosing Not to Hold Someone's Sin Against Him or Her Anymore

It is common for bitter people to bring up past offenses with those who have hurt them. They want them to feel as bad as they do! But we must let go of the past and choose to reject any thought of revenge. This doesn't mean you continue to put up with the abuse. God does not tolerate sin and neither should you. You will need to set up scriptural boundaries that put a stop to further abuse. Take a stand against sin while continuing to exercise grace and forgiveness toward those who hurt you. If you need help setting scriptural boundaries to protect yourself from further abuse, talk to a trusted friend, counselor, or pastor.

Don't Wait Until You Feel Like Forgiving

You will never get there. Make the hard choice to forgive even if you don't feel like it. Once you choose to forgive, Satan will lose his hold on you, and God will heal your damaged emotions.

Starting with the first person on your list, make the choice to forgive him or her for every painful memory that comes to your mind. Stay with that individual until you are sure you have dealt with all the remembered pain. Then work your way down the list in the same way.

As you begin forgiving people, God may bring to your mind painful memories you've totally forgotten. Let Him do this even if it hurts. God is bringing those painful memories to the surface so you can face them once for all time and let them go. Don't excuse the offender's behavior, even if it is someone you are really close to.

Don't say, "Lord, please help me to forgive." He is already helping you and will be with you all the way through the process. Don't say, "Lord, I want to forgive," because that bypasses the hard choice we have to make. Say, "Lord, I choose to forgive these people and what they did to me."

For every painful memory that God reveals for each person on your list, pray aloud if you are alone, or silently if in a group:

> *Lord Jesus, I choose to forgive (name the person) for (what they did or failed to do), because it made me feel (share the painful feelings—that is, rejected, dirty, worthless, inferior, and so on).*

After you have forgiven every person for every painful memory, then pray aloud and in unison as follows:

> *Lord Jesus, I choose not to hold on to my resentment. I relinquish my right to seek revenge and ask You to heal my damaged emotions. Thank You for setting me free from the bondage of my bitterness. I now ask You to bless those who have hurt me. In Jesus' name I pray. Amen.*

Before we came to Christ, thoughts were raised up in our minds against a true knowledge of God (2 Corinthians 10:3-5). Even as believers, we have harbored resentments toward God and that will hinder our walk with Him. We should have a healthy fear of God (awe of His holiness, power, and presence), but we fear no punishment from Him. Romans 8:15 reads, "You have not received a spirit of slavery leading to fear again, but you have received a spirit of adoption as sons by which we cry out, 'Abba! Father!'"

Step 4: Rebellion vs. Submission

We live in rebellious times. Many people sit in judgment of those in authority over them, and they submit only when it is convenient, or they do so in the fear of being caught. The Bible instructs us to pray for those in authority over us (1 Timothy 2:1-2), and to submit to governing authorities (Romans 13:1-7). Rebelling against God and His established authority leaves us spiritually vulnerable. The only time God permits us to disobey earthly leaders is when they require us to do something morally wrong, or attempt to rule outside the realm of their authority. To have a submissive spirit and a servant's heart, pray the following prayer aloud:

> *Dear heavenly Father, You have said that rebellion is as the sin of witchcraft, and insubordination is as iniquity and idolatry. I know that I have not always been submissive, but instead have rebelled in my heart against You and against those You have placed in authority over me in attitude and in action. Please show me all the ways I have been rebellious. I choose now to adopt a submissive spirit and a servant's heart. In Jesus' name I pray. Amen.*

It is an act of faith to trust God to work in our lives through something less than perfect leaders, but that is what God is asking us to do. Should those in positions of leadership or power abuse their authority and break the laws designed to protect innocent people, you need to seek help from a higher authority. Many states require certain types of abuse to be reported to a governmental agency. If that is your situation, we urge you to get the help you need immediately. Don't, however, assume an authority is violating God's Word just because he or she is telling you to do something you don't like. God has set up specific lines of authority to protect us and give order to society. It is the position of authority we respect. Without governing authorities every society would be chaos.

In the list below, allow the Lord to show you any specific ways you have been rebellious and use the prayer following to confess those sins He brings to mind.

- ☐ Civil government (including traffic laws, tax laws, attitude toward government officials) (Romans 13:1-7; 1 Timothy 2:1-4; 1 Peter 2:13-17)
- ☐ Parents, stepparents, or legal guardians (Ephesians 6:1-3)
- ☐ Teachers, coaches, school officials (Romans 13:1-4)
- ☐ Employers (past and present) (1 Peter 2:18-23)
- ☐ Husband (1 Peter 3:1-4) or wife (Ephesians 5:21; 1 Peter 3:7) (*Note to husbands:* Ask the Lord if your lack of love for your wife could be fostering a rebellious spirit within her. If so, confess that as a violation of Ephesians 5:22-33.)
- ☐ Church leaders (Hebrews 13:7)
- ☐ God (Daniel 9:5,9)

For each way in which the Spirit of God brings to your mind that you have been rebellious, use the following prayer to specifically confess that sin:

> *Lord Jesus, I confess that I have been rebellious toward (name or position) by (specifically confess what you did or did not do). Thank You for Your forgiveness. I choose to be submissive and obedient to Your Word. In Jesus' name I pray. Amen.*

Step 5: Pride vs. Humility

Pride comes before a fall, but God gives grace to the humble (James 4:6; 1 Peter 5:1-10). Humility is confidence properly placed in God, and we are instructed to "put no confidence in the flesh" (Philippians 3:3). We are to be "strong in the Lord and in the strength of His might" (Ephesians 6:10). Proverbs 3:5-7 urges us to trust in the Lord with all our hearts and not lean on our own understanding. Use the following prayer to ask for God's guidance concerning where you may be prideful:.

> *Dear heavenly Father, You have said that pride goes before destruction and an arrogant spirit before stumbling. I confess that I have focused on my own needs and desires and not others. I have not always denied myself, picked up my cross daily, and followed You. I have relied on my own strength and resources instead of resting in Yours. I have placed my will before Yours and centered my life around myself instead of You.*
>
> *I confess my pride and selfishness and pray that all ground gained in my life by the enemies of the Lord Jesus Christ would be canceled. I choose to rely upon the Holy Spirit's power and guidance so that I will do nothing from selfishness or empty conceit. With humility of mind, I choose to regard others as more important than myself. I acknowledge You as my Lord, and confess that apart from You I can do nothing of lasting significance.*
>
> *Please examine my heart and show me the specific ways I have lived my life in pride. In the gentle and humble name of Jesus I pray. Amen.*
>
> (See Proverbs 16:18; Matthew 6:33;
16:24; Romans 12:10; Philippians 2:3.)

Pray through the list below and use the prayer following to confess any sins of pride the Lord brings to mind.

- ☐ Having a stronger desire to do my will than God's will
- ☐ Leaning too much on my own understanding and experience rather than seeking God's guidance through prayer and His Word
- ☐ Relying on my own strengths and resources instead of depending on the power of the Holy Spirit
- ☐ Being more concerned about controlling others than developing self-control

- [ ] Being too busy doing "important" and selfish things rather than seeking and doing God's will
- [ ] Having a tendency to think I have no needs
- [ ] Finding it hard to admit when I am wrong
- [ ] Being more concerned about pleasing people than pleasing God
- [ ] Being overconcerned about getting the credit I feel I deserve
- [ ] Thinking I am more humble, spiritual, religious, or devoted than others
- [ ] Being driven to obtain recognition by attaining degrees, titles, and positions
- [ ] Often feeling that my needs are more important than another person's needs
- [ ] Considering myself better than others because of my academic, artistic, or athletic abilities and accomplishments
- [ ] Having feelings of inferiority appearing as false humility
- [ ] Not waiting on God
- [ ] Other ways I have thought more highly of myself than I should

For each of the above areas that has been true in your life, pray aloud if you are alone or silently if in a group:

> *Lord Jesus, I agree I have been proud by (<u>name what you checked above</u>). Thank You for Your forgiveness. I choose to humble myself before You and others. I choose to place all my confidence in You and put no confidence in my flesh. In Jesus' name I pray. Amen.*

Step 6: Bondage vs. Freedom

Many times we feel trapped in a vicious cycle of "sin-confess-sin-confess" that never seems to end. We can become very discouraged and end up just giving up and giving in to the sins of the flesh. In order to experience our freedom we must follow James 4:7: "Submit therefore to God. Resist the devil and he will flee from you." We submit to God by confession of sin and repentance (turning away from sin). We resist the devil by rejecting his lies. We must walk in the truth and put on the full armor of God (see Ephesians 6:10-20).

Sin that has become a habit often may require help from a trusted brother or sister in Christ. James 5:16 says, "Confess your sins to one another, and pray for one another, so that you may be healed. The effective prayer of a righteous man can accomplish much." Sometimes the assurance of 1 John 1:9 is enough: "If we confess our sins, He is faithful and righteous to forgive us our sins and to cleanse us from all unrighteousness."

Remember, confession is not saying, "I'm sorry." It is openly admitting, "I did it." Whether you need help from other people or just the accountability of walking in the light before God, pray the following prayer aloud:

> Dear heavenly Father, You have told me to put on the Lord Jesus Christ and make no provision for the flesh in regard to its lust. I confess that I have given in to fleshly lusts that wage war against my soul. I thank You that in Christ my sins are already forgiven, but I have broken Your holy law and I have allowed sin to wage war in my body. I come to You now to confess and renounce these sins of the flesh so that I might be cleansed and set free from the bondage of sin. Please reveal to my mind all the sins of the flesh I have committed and the ways I have grieved the Holy Spirit. In Jesus' holy name I pray. Amen.
>
> (See Romans 6:12-13; 13:14; 2 Corinthians 4:2;
> James 4:1; 1 Peter 2:11; 5:8.)

The following list contains many sins of the flesh, but a prayerful examination of Mark 7:20-23, Galatians 5:19-21, Ephesians 4:25-31, and other Scripture passages will help you to be even more thorough. Look over the list below and the Scriptures just listed and ask the

Holy Spirit to bring to your mind the sins you need to confess. He may reveal others to you as well. For each one the Lord shows you, pray a prayer of confession from your heart. There is a sample prayer following the list. (*Note:* Sexual sins, eating disorders, substance abuse, abortion, suicidal tendencies, and perfectionism will be dealt with later in this step.)*

> *Lord Jesus, I confess that I have sinned against You by (<u>name the</u>*
> <u>*sins*</u>*). Thank You for Your forgiveness and cleansing. I now turn*
> *away from these expressions of sin and turn to You, Lord. Fill*
> *me with Your Holy Spirit so that I will not carry out the desires*
> *of the flesh. In Jesus' name I pray. Amen.*

☐ Stealing

☐ Swearing

☐ Cheating

☐ Quarreling/fighting

☐ Apathy/laziness

☐ Procrastination

☐ Jealousy/envy

☐ Lying

☐ Greed/materialism

☐ Complaining/criticism

☐ Hatred

☐ Sarcasm

☐ Anger

☐ Lustful actions

☐ Lustful thoughts

☐ Gossip/slander

☐ Drunkenness

Others:

☐ _____

☐ _____

☐ _____

☐ _____

Resolving Sexual Sin

It is our responsibility not to allow sin to reign (rule) in our mortal bodies. We must not use our bodies or another person's body as an instrument of unrighteousness (see Romans 6:12-13). Sexual immorality is a sin not only against God, but against your body, the temple of the Holy

---

* If you are struggling with habitual sin, read *Overcoming Addictive Behavior* (Regal Books, 2003).

Spirit (1 Corinthians 6:18-19). To find freedom from sexual bondage, begin by praying the following prayer:

> *Lord Jesus, I have allowed sin to reign in my mortal body. I ask You to bring to my mind every sexual use of my body as an instrument of unrighteousness so that I can renounce these sexual sins and break those sinful bondages. In Jesus' name I pray. Amen.*

As the Lord brings to your mind every immoral sexual use of your body, whether it was done to you (rape, incest, sexual molestation) or willingly by you (pornography, masturbation, sexual immorality), renounce *every* experience as follows:

> *Lord Jesus, I renounce (<u>name the sexual experience</u>) with (<u>name</u>). I ask You to break that sinful bond with (<u>name</u>) spiritually, physically, and emotionally.*

After you are finished, commit your body to the Lord by praying:

> *Lord Jesus, I renounce all these uses of my body as an instrument of unrighteousness, and I admit to any willful participation. I choose to present my physical body to You as an instrument of righteousness, a living and holy sacrifice, acceptable to You. I choose to reserve the sexual use of my body for marriage only. I reject the devil's lie that my body is not clean or that it is dirty or in any way unacceptable to You as a result of my past sexual experiences. Lord, thank You that You have cleansed and forgiven me and that You love and accept me just the way I am. Therefore, I choose now to accept myself and my body as clean in Your eyes. In Jesus' name I pray. Amen.*

Pray the following prayers out loud where they are applicable to you, whether alone or in a group:

PORNOGRAPHY:

> *Lord Jesus, I confess that I have looked at sexually suggestive and pornographic material for the purpose of stimulating myself*

sexually. I have attempted to satisfy my lustful desires and polluted my body, soul, and spirit. Thank You for cleansing me and for Your forgiveness. I renounce any satanic bonds I have allowed in my life through the unrighteous use of my body and mind. Lord, I commit myself to destroy any objects in my possession that I have used for sexual stimulation, and to turn away from all media that are associated with my sexual sin. I commit myself to the renewing of my mind and to think pure thoughts. Fill me with Your Holy Spirit that I may not carry out the desires of the flesh. In Jesus' name I pray. Amen.

HOMOSEXUALITY:

Heavenly Father, I renounce the lie that You have created me or anyone else to be homosexual, and I agree that in Your Word You clearly forbid homosexual behavior. I choose to accept myself as a child of God, and I thank You that You created me as a man (woman). I renounce all homosexual thoughts, urges, drives, and acts and renounce all ways in which Satan has used these things to pervert my relationships. I announce that I am free in Christ to relate to the opposite sex and my own sex in the way that You intended. In Jesus' name I pray. Amen.

ABORTION:

Lord Jesus, I confess that I was not a proper guardian and keeper of the life You entrusted to me, and I confess that I have sinned. Thank You that because of Your forgiveness, I can forgive myself. I commit the child to You for all eternity, and believe that he or she is in Your caring hands. In Jesus' name I pray. Amen.

SUICIDAL TENDENCIES:

Heavenly Father, I renounce all suicidal thoughts and any attempts I've made to take my own life or in any way injure myself. I renounce the lie that life is hopeless and that I can find peace and freedom by taking my own life. Satan is a thief and comes to steal, kill, and destroy. I choose life in Christ, who said

He came to give me life and give it abundantly. Thank You for Your forgiveness, which allows me to forgive myself. I choose to believe that there is always hope in Christ and that You love me. In Jesus' name I pray. Amen.

DRIVENNESS AND PERFECTIONISM:

Heavenly Father, I renounce the lie that my sense of worth is dependent upon my ability to perform. I announce the truth that my identity and sense of worth is found in who I am as Your child. I renounce seeking the approval and acceptance of other people, and I choose to believe I am already approved and accepted in Christ because of His death and resurrection for me. I choose to believe the truth I have been saved, not by deeds done in righteousness, but according to Your mercy. I choose to believe I am no longer under the curse of the law, because Christ became a curse for me. I receive the free gift of life in Christ and choose to abide in Him. I renounce striving for perfection by living under the law. By Your grace, heavenly Father, I choose from this day forward to walk by faith in the power of Your Holy Spirit according to what You have said is true. In Jesus' name I pray. Amen.

EATING DISORDERS OR SELF-MUTILATION:

Heavenly Father, I renounce the lie that my value as a person is dependent upon my appearance or performance. I renounce cutting or abusing myself, vomiting, using laxatives, or starving myself as a means of being in control, altering my appearance, or trying to cleanse myself of evil. I announce that only the blood of the Lord Jesus Christ cleanses me from sin. I realize that I have been bought with a price and that my body, the temple of the Holy Spirit, belongs to God. Therefore, I choose to glorify God in my body. I renounce the lie that I am evil or that any part of my body is evil. Thank You that You accept me just the way I am in Christ. In Jesus' name I pray. Amen.

SUBSTANCE ABUSE:

Heavenly Father, I confess I have misused substances (alcohol, tobacco, food, prescription or street drugs) for the purpose of pleasure, to escape reality, or to cope with difficult problems. I confess I have abused my body and programmed my mind in harmful ways. I have quenched the Holy Spirit as well. Thank You for Your forgiveness. I renounce any satanic connection or influence in my life through my misuse of food or chemicals. I cast my anxieties onto Christ, who loves me. I commit myself to yield no longer to substance abuse, but instead I choose to allow the Holy Spirit to direct and empower me. In Jesus' name I pray. Amen.

Step 7: Curses vs. Blessings

Scripture declares that the iniquities of one generation can be visited onto the third and fourth generations, but God's blessings will be poured out on thousands of generations of those who love and obey Him (Exodus 20:4-6). The iniquities of one generation can adversely affect future ones unless those sins are renounced and our new spiritual heritage in Christ is claimed.

This cycle of abuse and all negative influences can be stopped through genuine repentance. Jesus died for your sins, but this is appropriated only when you choose to believe Him and experienced only when you repent. You are not guilty of your ancestors' sins, but because of their sins you were affected by their influence. Jesus said that after we have been fully trained, we will be like our teachers (Luke 6:40), and Peter wrote that we were redeemed from our futile way of life inherited from our forefathers (1 Peter 1:18). Ask the Lord to reveal your ancestral sins and then renounce them as follows:

Dear heavenly Father, please reveal to my mind all the sins of my ancestors that have been passed down through family lines. Since I am a new creation in Christ, I want to experience my freedom from those influences and walk in my new identity as a child of God. In Jesus' name I pray. Amen.

Lord, I renounce (confess all the family sins that God brings to your mind).

Satan and people may curse us, but it will not have any effect on us unless we believe it. We cannot passively take our place in Christ—we must actively and intentionally choose to submit to God and resist the devil, and then he will flee from us. Complete this final step with the following declaration and prayer:

DECLARATION:

I here and now reject and disown all the sins of my ancestors. As one who has been delivered from the domain of darkness and transferred into the kingdom of God's Son, I declare myself to be free from those harmful influences. I am no longer "in Adam." I am now alive "in Christ." Therefore I am the recipient of the blessings of God upon my life as I choose to love and obey Him.

As one who has been crucified and raised with Christ and who sits with Him in heavenly places, I renounce any and all satanic attacks and assignments directed against me and my ministry. Every curse placed on me was broken when Christ became a curse for me by dying on the cross (Galatians 3:13). I reject any and every way in which Satan may claim ownership of me. I belong to the Lord Jesus Christ who purchased me with His own precious blood. I declare myself to be fully and eternally signed over and committed to the Lord Jesus Christ.

Therefore, having submitted to God and by His authority, I now resist the devil, and I command every spiritual enemy of the Lord Jesus Christ to leave my presence. I put on the armor of God, and I stand against Satan's temptations, accusations, and deceptions. From this day forward I will seek to do only the will of my heavenly Father.

PRAYER:

Dear heavenly Father, I come to You as Your child, bought out of slavery to sin by the blood of the Lord Jesus Christ. You are the Lord of the universe and the Lord of my life. I submit my body to You as a living and holy sacrifice. May You be glorified through my life and body. I now ask You to fill me with Your

Holy Spirit. I commit myself to the renewing of my mind in order that I may prove that Your will is good, acceptable, and perfect for me. I desire nothing more than to be like You. I pray, believe, and do all this in the wonderful name of Jesus, my Lord and Savior. Amen.

Maintaining Your Freedom

It is exciting to experience your freedom in Christ, but what you have gained must be maintained. You have won an important battle, but the war goes on. To maintain your freedom in Christ and grow in the grace of God, you must continue renewing your mind to the truth of God's Word. If you become aware of lies you have believed, renounce them and choose the truth. If more painful memories surface, then forgive those who hurt you and renounce any sinful part you played. Many people choose to go through the Steps to Freedom in Christ again on their own to make sure they have dealt with all their issues. Oftentimes new issues will surface, and the process can assist you in a regular "housecleaning."*

It is not uncommon that after going though the Steps, people have thoughts like: *Nothing has really changed. You're the same person you always were. It didn't work.* In most cases you should just ignore them. We are not called to dispel the darkness—we are called to turn on the light. You don't get rid of negative thoughts by rebuking every one. Rather, you get rid of them by repenting and choosing the truth.

I encourage you to read *Victory over the Darkness* and *The Bondage Breaker* if you haven't already done so. To continue growing in the grace of God I suggest the following:

1. Get rid of or destroy any cult or occult objects in your home. (See Acts 19:18-20.)

2. Get involved in a small-group ministry where you can be

---

* The book *Restored* (e3 Resources, 2007) is an expanded and illustrated version of the Steps to Freedom, which is very helpful for those going through the Steps alone or for those who want to go through the Steps again on their own.

a real person, and be part of a church where God's truth is taught with kindness and grace.

3. Read and meditate on the truth of God's Word each day.

4. Don't let your mind be passive, especially concerning what you watch and listen to (music, TV, and so on). Actively take every thought captive to the obedience of Christ.

5. Learn to pray by the Spirit.*

6. Remember, you are responsible for your mental, spiritual, and physical health.†

7. Work through *The Daily Discipler* (Regal Books, 2005), a discipleship book that takes you through the sanctifying process for five days a week over the period of a year.

DAILY PRAYER AND DECLARATION:

Dear heavenly Father, I praise You and honor You as my Lord and Savior. You are in control of all things. I thank You that You are always with me and will never leave me nor forsake me. You are the only all-powerful and only wise God. You are kind and loving in all Your ways. I love You and thank You that I am united with Christ and spiritually alive in Him. I choose not to love the world or the things in the world, and I crucify the flesh and all its passions.

Thank You for the life I now have in Christ. I ask You to fill me with the Holy Spirit so I can be guided by You and not carry out the desires of the flesh. I declare my total dependence upon You, and I take my stand against Satan and all his lying ways. I choose to believe the truth of Your Word despite what my feelings may say. I refuse to be discouraged; You are the God of all hope. Nothing is too difficult for You. I am confident that You will supply all my needs as I seek to live according to Your Word. I

---

* See *Praying by the Power of the Spirit* (Harvest House, 2003).

† In regard to your physical health, see *The Biblical Guide to Alternative Medicine* (Regal Books, 2003).

thank You I can be content and live a responsible life through Christ who strengthens me.

I now take my stand against Satan and command him and all his evil spirits to depart from me. I choose to put on the full armor of God so I may be able to stand firm against all the devil's schemes. I submit my body as a living and holy sacrifice to You, and I choose to renew my mind by Your living Word. By so doing I will be able to prove that Your will is good, acceptable, and perfect for me. In the name of my Lord and Savior, Jesus Christ I pray. Amen.

BEDTIME PRAYER:

Thank You, Lord, that You have brought me into Your family and have blessed me with every spiritual blessing in the heavenly places in Christ Jesus. Thank You for this time of renewal and refreshment through sleep. I accept it as one of Your blessings for Your children, and I trust You to guard my mind and my body during my sleep.

As I have thought about You and Your truth during the day, I choose to let those good thoughts continue in my mind while I am asleep. I commit myself to You for Your protection against every attempt of Satan and his demons to attack me during sleep. Guard my mind from nightmares. I renounce all fear and cast every anxiety upon You, Lord. I commit myself to You as my rock, my fortress, and my strong tower. May Your peace be upon this place of rest. In the strong name of the Lord Jesus Christ I pray. Amen.

PRAYER FOR SPIRITUAL CLEANSING OF HOME/APARTMENT/ROOM:

After removing and destroying all objects of false worship, pray this prayer aloud in every room:

Heavenly Father, I acknowledge that You are the Lord of heaven and earth. In Your sovereign power and love, You have entrusted me with many things. Thank You for this place to live. I claim my home as a place of spiritual safety for me and my family and ask for Your protection from all the attacks of the enemy.

As a child of God, raised up and seated with Christ in the heavenly places, I command every evil spirit claiming ground in this place, based on the activities of past or present occupants, including me and my family, to leave and never return. I renounce all demonic assignments directed against this place. I ask You, heavenly Father, to post Your holy angels around this place to guard it from any and all attempts of the enemy to enter and disturb Your purposes for me and my family. I thank You, Lord, for doing this in the name of the Lord Jesus Christ. Amen.

PRAYER FOR LIVING IN A NON-CHRISTIAN ENVIRONMENT:

After removing and destroying all objects of false worship from your possession, pray this aloud in the place where you live:

Thank You, heavenly Father, for a place to live and to be renewed by sleep. I ask You to set aside my room (or portion of this room) as a place of spiritual safety for me. I renounce any allegiance given to false gods or spirits by other occupants. I renounce any claim to this room (space) by Satan based on the activities of past or present occupants, including me. On the basis of my position as a child of God and joint-heir with Christ, who has all authority in heaven and on earth, I command all evil spirits to leave this place and never return. I ask You, heavenly Father, to station Your holy angels to protect me while I live here. In Jesus' mighty name I pray. Amen.

The apostle Paul prays in Ephesians 1:18,

I pray that the eyes of your heart may be enlightened, so that you will know what is the hope of His calling, what are the riches of the glory of His inheritance in the saints, and what is the surpassing greatness of His power toward us who believe.

Beloved, you are a child of God (1 John 3:1-3), and "My God will supply all your needs according to His riches in glory in Christ

Jesus" (Philippians 4:19). Your critical needs are the *being* needs such as eternal or spiritual life, which He has given you, and an identity, which you have "in Christ." In addition, Jesus has met your needs for *acceptance, security,* and *significance.* Memorize and meditate on the following truths daily.* Read the entire list aloud, morning and evening, for the next few weeks. Think about what you are reading, and let the truth of who you are in Christ renew your mind. This is your inheritance in Christ.

In Christ

I renounce the lie that I am rejected, unloved, or shameful. In Christ I am accepted. God says...

> I am God's child (John 1:12)
>
> I am Christ's friend (John 15:5)
>
> I have been justified (Romans 5:1)
>
> I am united with the Lord and I am one spirit with Him (1 Corinthians 6:17)
>
> I have been bought with a price: I belong to God (1 Corinthians 6:19-20)
>
> I am a member of Christ's body (1 Corinthians 12:27)
>
> I am a saint, a holy one (Ephesians 1:1)
>
> I have been adopted as God's child (Ephesians 1:5)
>
> I have direct access to God through the Holy Spirit (Ephesians 2:18)
>
> I have been redeemed and forgiven of all my sins (Colossians 1:14)
>
> I am complete in Christ (Colossians 2:10)

I renounce the lie that I am guilty, unprotected, alone, or abandoned. In Christ I am secure. God says...

> I am free from condemnation (Romans 8:1-2)

---

* These can be found in the devotional *Who I Am in Christ* (Regal Books, 2001).

I am assured that all things work together for good (Romans 8:28)

I am free from any condemning charges against me (Romans 8:31-34)

I cannot be separated from the love of God (Romans 8:35-39)

I have been established, anointed, and sealed by God (2 Corinthians 1:21-22)

I am confident that the good work God has begun in me will be perfected (Philippians 1:6)

I am a citizen of heaven (Philippians 3:20)

I am hidden with Christ in God (Colossians 3:3)

I have not been given a spirit of fear, but of power, love, and discipline (2 Timothy 1:7)

I can find grace and mercy to help in time of need (Hebrews 4:16)

I am born of God and the evil one cannot touch me (1 John 5:18)

I renounce the lie that I am worthless, inadequate, helpless, or hopeless. In Christ I am significant. God says...

I am the salt of the earth and the light of the world (Matthew 5:13-14)

I am a branch of the true vine, Jesus, a channel of His life (John 15:1,5)

I have been chosen and appointed by God to bear fruit (John 15:16)

I am a personal, Spirit-empowered witness of Christ's (Acts 1:8)

I am a temple of God (1 Corinthians 3:16)

I am a minister of reconciliation for God (2 Corinthians 5:17-21)

I am God's co-worker (2 Corinthians 6:1)

I am seated with Christ in the heavenly realm (Ephesians 2:6)

I am God's workmanship, created for good works (Ephesians 2:10)

I may approach God with freedom and confidence (Ephesians 3:12)

I can do all things through Christ who strengthens me! (Philippians 4:13)

I am not the great "I Am,"
but by the grace of God I am what I am.

(See Exodus 3:14; John 8:24,28,58; 1 Corinthians 15:10.)

10

DISCIPLESHIP COUNSELING

When I was still teaching at Talbot School of Theology, a professional Christian counselor attended a one-week intensive class that I offered on resolving personal and spiritual conflicts. He told me that in 15 years of counseling he had never seen any cases that involved spiritual warfare. However, he had been reading about the New Age movement and felt he had better be prepared in case the enemy did show up in one of his clients. A month later he wrote me a letter. After the course he went back to his practice and found out that every one of his clients was being deceived and so was he.

Don't Ignore the Spiritual Battle

Why didn't this counselor recognize this battle for their minds before? There are two reasons why the spiritual battle is overlooked in the Western world. First, the contemporary Western world is dominated by rationalism and naturalism. The symptoms of spiritual warefare are present, but they are explained another way. Every psychologist, psychiatrist, and professional counselor has clients who are hearing voices or are plagued by tempting, condemning, blasphemous, or suicidal thoughts. The vast majority of people who are incarcerated and those who are struggling in recovery groups are also struggling with their thoughts and hearing voices. In such groups it is common to hear the following: "Don't pay attention to that committee in your head," and "You have to get rid of that stinking thinking."

The secular world usually explains those symptoms as a chemical imbalance. But how can a chemical produce a personality or a thought? Or how can our neurotransmitters randomly fire in such a way so as to create a thought we are opposed to thinking? The secularist would likely respond by saying, "When such people are given antipsychotic medication, the voices stop." Yes, and so does almost everything else. Remove the medication, and you are back to where you were before. That doesn't solve anything. It just narcotizes the symptoms, which is what alcoholics and addicts do when they use chemicals. They have no mental peace, so they drown out their thoughts with alcohol and drugs.

Second, many counselors will never see the spiritual conflict because they have not been taught how to *resolve* anything. They have been taught to *explain* people's pathology and help them learn coping skills. The devil will raise no opposition to that. Most pastors and Christian leaders won't see any spiritual opposition either if all they are doing is running programs, teaching, and preaching. They will, however, come across spiritual opposition when they get personally involved with their parishioners and help them work toward resolution.

I am certainly not suggesting a deliverance ministry that considers only the demonic. What is needed is a wholistic answer from God's perspective. People have spiritual, mental, emotional, and physical problems, and God relates to us as whole people. He takes into account all of reality all of the time. I believe Scripture speaks directly to our physical, psychological, and spiritual issues, and I have done my best to write extensively on most of them from a biblical worldview perspective. I also believe that the world and its inhabitants are in this mess because of the Fall, and our only hope is to get back into a righteous relationship with God under the New Covenant of grace. Jesus says, "The time is fulfilled, and the kingdom of God is at hand; repent and believe the gospel" (Mark 1:15). What seems to be lacking in the church all over the world is opportunities for people to repent.

Most Christians and seekers are coming to our churches with a lot of unresolved issues. They come in with their baggage, hear a good message, and go home with the same baggage. Churches need to be equipped to help them resolve their personal and spiritual conflicts through genuine repentance and faith in God. But where do we start? That is the most common question we get asked by church leaders.

Resources for Resolving Personal and Spiritual Conflicts

Freedom in Christ Ministries began with my books and expanded into a conference ministry with the Living Free in Christ conference. To that we added training for Discipleship Counseling.

The Living Free in Christ conference is now available as a curriculum for Sunday schools, small groups, home Bible studies, and other venues. It is entitled "The Freedom in Christ Course" in the United States and "The Freedom in Christ Discipleship Course" in the United Kingdom.

Both courses include a DVD with messages for each lesson and a teacher's guide that has all the messages written out so leaders can choose to give the message themselves or play the DVD. The "Learner's Guide" for the courses includes the Steps to Freedom in Christ. (Each participant should have a copy of the Learner's Guide.)

This course is the entry point for churches, but it is not an end. Hopefully, for most people it will be a new beginning on their journey to freedom and wholeness. If there are no additional issues they have that need to be resolved, the *Daily Discipler* is a good follow-up. It is written to give believers a practical theology that can be digested five days a week for a year.

The next step is to help marriage partners become one in Christ. The book for that is *Experiencing Christ Together*, which has "Steps for Beginning Your Marriage Free" and "Steps for Setting Your Marriage Free." The book and the "Steps for Beginning Your Marriage Free" are intended for premarital counseling; the book and the "Steps for Setting Your Marriage Free" are for Sunday school classes and small-group studies. (There are modified Steps available when only one partner will try.)

These marriage steps follow the same reasoning as the individual

Steps to Freedom in Christ—that is, that the presence of God is integral to the process. It usually takes a full day for couples to work through it. We recommend that first the book be read, taught, or both. Then schedule the process of the Steps for a weekend at church or somewhere else. This powerful process helps couples resolve their conflicts by the grace of God.

The final step is for the official board of the church and the ministerial staff to resolve the church's conflicts and set the church or ministry free. The book for that is *Extreme Church Makeover,* which explains servant leadership and lays the foundation for corporate conflict resolution. The "Steps to Setting Your Church Free" are a process that the board and staff work through. It usually requires a day and an evening to do this.

The marriage and church steps cannot be processed without individual freedom being established first. That is why the "Freedom in Christ Course" should be offered first for individuals, couples, and leaders. If you have a church full of people in bondage to sex, alcohol, drugs, bitterness, gambling, legalism, and so on, you have a *church* in bondage. If you have a church full of bad marriages, you have a bad church. The whole cannot be greater than the sum of its parts.

I have also written a book entitled *Restored,* which is an expansion upon the Steps to Freedom in Christ with further explanation and illustrations. Many Christians can work through this book on their own and facilitate their own repentance. That is possible since God is the Wonderful Counselor and the One who grants repentance.

Why Are the Steps to Freedom Needed?

Many Christians are left on their own to resolve their personal and spiritual conflicts through repentance and faith in God, and the vast majority don't fully understand how to do that. I didn't either during my early years of ministry.*

A major shift in my thinking took place when I realized there are more than two parties present in any given counseling session. God

---

* I expand on the reasoning behind the Steps to Freedom in the appendix.

is the third party, and He is present all the time. There is a role that God and only God can play in our lives and in the lives of those we are trying to help. Only God can set captives free and bind up their broken hearts. If I try to play the role of God in someone else's life, I will misdirect their struggle with God to myself, and I am not adequate for that task. If I leave God out, nothing of lasting consequence will happen. Jesus said, "I am the vine, you are the branches; he who abides in Me and I in him, he bears much fruit, for apart from Me you can do nothing" (John 15:5 NASB). That being the case, who is responsible for what?

A lot of literature discusses the role relationship between the encourager and the inquirer. Consequently, most pastors and counselors have been trained not to be rescuers, or enablers, or codependents, and they have learned how to set boundaries in the encourager–inquirer relationship. Many, however, have not been trained to include God in the counseling process. Keep in mind that we don't have to invoke God's presence, because He is omnipresent, but we do need to be consciously aware of His presence and what He has promised to do. Every counseling session has three participants, as illustrated below:

Hopefully there is an intimate relationship between the encourager and God. What remains to be established is a right relationship between the encourager and the inquirer as well as a right relationship between the inquirer and their heavenly Father. Each of the three has an important role to play that cannot be played by either of the other two without hindering the process.

The Sovereign Role of God

First, let's consider the sovereign role of God, which I often explain to those I am trying to help. In the course of living there is a precise line between God's sovereignty and mankind's responsibility, as shown below:

God's sovereignty	Our responsibility

We may draw the line further to the left or further to the right according to our theology, but most agree that God's sovereignty and mankind's responsibility are both taught in Scripture. Everything on the left side of the line is God's responsibility. If we try to do what only God can do, we will be frustrated and fail in our efforts. We are not the Creator, we can't save ourselves, we shouldn't try to be someone else's conscience, and we can't change another person. We can count on the fact that God will always be faithful to His Word and His covenant relationship with us.

The key to successful ministry is to know God and understand His ways:

> This is what the Lord says: "Let not the wise man boast of his wisdom or the strong man boast of his strength or the rich man boast of his riches, but let him who boasts boast about this: that he understands and knows me, that I am the LORD, who exercises kindness, justice and righteousness on earth, for in these I delight" (Jeremiah 9:23-24).

And Jesus is "the way and the truth and the life" (John 14:6). There is no other way, there is no other truth, and no one else can give us eternal life.

The Creator designed us to live a certain way. When we rebel against God and live another way it ends in defeat for Christians and spiritual death for non-Christians. "There is a way that seems right to a man, but in the end it leads to death" (Proverbs 14:12). To proclaim only "one way" invites scorn from non-Christians and pricks the pride of the self-sufficient.

WHY JUST ONE WAY?

Perhaps an analogy will illustrate why there can be only one way we're designed to live and why the concept relates not only to Christianity. Suppose you have just purchased a new computer whose hard drive is formatted differently from your old one. You want badly to use this new computer in the same way you used your old one, but you can't. To be effective you will have to learn a whole new way. The manufacturer designed that computer to work "one way." If you ignore the instruction book, you will be able to do very little with your computer. But if you master the manufacturer's handbook, you will be able to accomplish a lot with your computer. For the believer, God is the manufacturer and the Bible is the manufacturer's handbook, and if we study and apply it we can do all things through Christ who strengthens us.

Human Responsibility

On the other side of the line is our responsibility, which has been revealed in Scripture. God will not do for us what He has instructed us to do. In fact, He cannot. God can only do that which is consistent with His nature and His Word. For example, God cannot lie, and He will not deviate from His Word or His ways. "The grass withers and the flowers fall, but the word of our God stands forever" (Isaiah 40:8). The truth that God is immutable (unchangeable) is what gives us consistency in life. "Jesus Christ is the same yesterday and today and forever" (Hebrews 13:8). It will do no good to pray and ask God to think for us, when He has instructed us to think (1 Corinthians 14:20; Philippians 4:8). He will not believe for us, repent for us, forgive others for us, and so on—but He will enable us to do all that He has commanded us to do.

The devil has a field day when we don't understand this simple truth. We expect God to act a certain way, and when He doesn't, we are disappointed with Him. Or we pray and nothing happens. Chances are, "When you ask, you do not receive, because you ask with wrong motives" (James 4:3). Not knowing who is responsible for what is even more devastating when it comes to spiritual conflicts. Suppose a boy suddenly becomes aware of a spiritual presence in his room at night. He pulls the covers over his head and cries out, "God, do something!" God doesn't seem to do anything. So he questions, "Why don't you do something, God? You're all-powerful. You can make it go away. Maybe You don't care, or maybe I'm not a Christian. Maybe that is why You won't help me!" After such experiences, many people end up questioning God and their salvation.

"Why didn't God do something?" they ask. He did. He defeated the devil and positioned the church with His authority over the kingdom of darkness. Whose responsibility is it to resist the devil, put on the armor of God, and take every thought captive to the obedience of Christ? What if you don't do those things? Will God do them for you?

I have counseled many defeated Christians who have asked God to assume their responsibility for them in many subtle ways. Some have even hoped He would change or alter His ways just this one time in order to accommodate them. If He did, He would no longer be God. God will always stay true to His character and will always keep His word. Therefore we can claim His promises and rest in the finished work of Christ.

The Inquirer's Responsibility

There is one place in Scripture that explains what the sick or suffering are supposed to do. James 5:13-16 reads,

> Is anyone among you suffering? Then he must pray. Is anyone cheerful? He is to sing praises. Is anyone among you sick? Then he must call for the elders of the church and they are to pray over him, anointing him with oil in the name of the Lord; and the prayer offered in faith will restore the one who is sick, and the Lord will raise him up, and if he has committed sins, they will be forgiven him. Therefore, confess your sins to one another, and pray for one another so that you

may be healed. The effective prayer of a righteous man can accomplish much (NASB).

When this passage is considered, the focus is usually on the role of the elders, but what is often overlooked is the role and responsibility of the suffering and the sick. Our prayers for others will not be very effective if the following is overlooked.

WHO MUST PRAY

First, we cannot do another person's praying for them. Initially, the one who is suffering is the one who should be praying. I believe in intercessory prayer, but not for the purpose of replacing another person's responsibility to pray. The point is, I cannot do *your* praying for you.

In my early years of ministry, I would get stuck with most of the people I was trying to help, so I would stop and ask God for wisdom (see James 1:5). I was hoping God would give me the answer so I could share it with the person I was trying to help. I began to realize that would make me a medium! Paul wrote, "There is one God and one mediator between God and men, the man Christ Jesus" (1 Timothy 2:5). Rather than pray for them, I started to have *them* pray, and I underwent a radical shift in methodology.

To illustrate, suppose you have two sons. The younger brother is always asking his older brother to talk to you for him. Would you accept that as a parent? Can you have a secondhand relationship with one of your children? Can we with God? This paradigm shift resulted in the Steps to Freedom in Christ, in which the inquirer verbally prays and responds to God.

REVEALING DEEPER ISSUES

Second, most inquirers will present problems that are often symptoms of much deeper issues that need to be resolved, issues that God obviously knows. In the past I would have tried to help them resolve the problems they presented. Now I listen to their story and ask if they would like to seek resolution with God's help. They always say yes, and with their permission I lead them through the Steps to Freedom. When they pray, many other issues will surface that are critical in terms of their relationship with God. These will not likely show up with traditional methods of counseling. They may tell you about the one or two people they are struggling with. But when they pray and ask God to reveal to their minds who they need to forgive, many more names will come out. Have you helped them be fully reconciled to God if you dealt with only the one or two names or issues they volunteered to share? I doubt it.

That is why we don't have just a sex or alcohol or marriage problem. If the answer is to get back into a righteous relationship with God, then we need to consider *all* the issues that are impeding us from having an intimate relationship with our heavenly Father. You will not enlist God's help in overcoming lust if you hang on to your pride, because God is opposed to the proud. If you hold on to your bitterness and refuse to forgive, God will turn you over to the tormentors, which is a disciplinary action. He doesn't want His children to live in the bondage of bitterness. Bitterness is like swallowing poison, hoping the other person will die.

REPENTANCE IN ACTION

Let's apply this methodology to what we learned in chapter 5 of this book. Recall that Romans 6:11 explains our position in Christ and teaches that we should consider ourselves to be alive in Christ and dead to sin. Verse 12 explains that it is our responsibility to not let sin reign in our mortal bodies. The next verse teaches how we can avoid that. We are not to use our bodies as instruments of unrighteousness, but instead present ourselves to God as those alive from the dead and our bodies as instruments of righteousness.

Given that understanding, we have the inquirers pray and ask the Lord to reveal to their minds every sexual use of their bodies as instruments of unrighteousness—and God does. Additionally, 1 Corinthians 6 teaches that our bodies are temples of God and we are not to join ourselves sexually with a harlot, else we will become one flesh.

Such bonding needs to be resolved. As God brings sexual experiences to their minds, we have them renounce each sexual experience and ask God to break the "one flesh" bond that may exist between them and their other partners. They conclude by presenting their bodies to God as a living sacrifice (Romans 12:1), which makes possible the process of renewing their minds (Romans 12:2).

The only effective prayer at this stage is the prayer of a repentant heart. Chances are the inquirer's own attempts at prayer have not been effective. The psalmist explains why: "If I regard iniquity in my heart, the Lord will not hear me" (Psalm 66:18 KJV). The answer is to deal with the iniquity, not ask someone else to do your praying for you. Expecting a counselor or pastor to petition God for us is abdicating our responsibility, and it will not be as effective.

After I spoke in a Christian recovery conference, a licensed therapist who had been sexually abused asked me for help. Three hours later she was experiencing her freedom in Christ. At the door she paused and said, "I always thought someone else had to pray for me." That belief is commonly held by many pastors and counselors as well as those they are trying to help. I have learned to put that responsibility back where it belongs, on the inquirer. Conviction of sin and divine guidance come directly from God to all His children. In the discipleship counseling process, the inquirer prays, and God responds to him or her. That is why we can process the Steps by ourselves, because the critical relationship is between us and our heavenly Father.

"The effective prayer of a righteous man can accomplish much" if the person we have prayed for has been willing to confess and get right with God, which is the order presented in the James passage quoted above. The role of the encourager is given in 2 Timothy 2:24-26:

> The Lord's servant must not quarrel; instead, he must be kind to everyone, able to teach, not resentful. Those who oppose him he must gently instruct, in the hope that God will grant repentance leading them to a knowledge of the truth, and that they will come to their senses and escape the trap of the devil, who has taken them captive to do his will.

QUESTIONS FOR DISCUSSION AND THOUGHT

1. Read the research in the sidebar below. What are you now thinking? Why?

2. Why is it so important to understand the different roles, responsibilities, and limits of God, the encourager, and the inquirer?

3. How will Satan take advantage of our confusion over who is responsible for what?

4. Can you do another person's praying for them? Why or why not?

5. What is the role of the encourager?

THE EFFECTIVENESS OF THE STEPS TO FREEDOM IN CHRIST

There have been several studies that have shown promising results regarding the effectiveness of the Steps. Three of these studies were done in 1996 with people who attended "Living Free in Christ" conferences and were led through the Steps during them.* In each case, participants completed a questionnaire before working through the Steps. Three months afterward, these people filled out the same questionnaire again.† This table shows the percentage of improvement they experienced in five key categories.

---

* The "Living Free in Christ" conference is now available in a course entitled *Beta: The Next Step in Discipleship* (Gospel Light Publications, 2005).

† The studies were administered by Judith King, a Christian therapist. The first involved 30 participants who filled out a 10-item questionnaire; the second involved 55 participants who filled out a 12-item questionnaire; and the third involved 21 participants who also filled out a 12-item questionnaire.

	Depression	Anxiety	Inner Conflict	Tormenting Thoughts	Addictive Behavior
Study 1	64%	58%	63%	82%	52%
Study 2	47%	44%	51%	58%	43%
Study 3	52%	47%	48%	57%	39%

Most people attending a "Living Free in Christ" conference can work through the repentance process on their own using the Steps. In our experience, however, about 15 percent can't, because of difficulties they have experienced. A personal session with a trained encourager was offered to them. (I discuss encourager training in my book *Discipleship Counseling* from Regal Books, which explains the theology and methodology of this approach.)

At two conferences, people who had sessions with trained encouragers were given a pre-test before going through the Steps. They were then given a post-test three months later,* which showed the following improvements in seven key categories:

	Conference 1	Conference 2
Depression	44%	57%
Anxiety	45%	54%
Fear	48%	49%
Anger	36%	55%
Tormenting Thoughts	51%	50%
Negative Habits	48%	53%
Sense of Self-Worth	52%	56%

* This research was conducted by the Board of the Ministry of Healing in Tyler, Texas. The board is chaired by Dr. George Hurst, formerly director of the University of Texas at Tyler Health Center (george.hurst@uthct.edu). Conference 1 took place in Oklahoma City, Oklahoma; Conference 2 took place in Tyler, Texas. The Tyler, Texas, study was carried out by a doctoral student at Regent University under the supervision of Fernando Garzon, Doctor of Psychology.

Appendix

THE RATIONALE
FOR THE STEPS TO
FREEDOM IN CHRIST

In the last 40 years, North American culture has shifted dramatically. An increasing number of Christians struggle with addictive behaviors related to food, gambling, alcohol, drugs, and sex. The vast majority of those seeking treatment for a chemical addiction are also sexually addicted, which will probably not be addressed. Fifty percent of the general population in their twenties has a sexually transmitted disease, and the availability of pornography on the Internet has captured many in the web of lust.

The disintegration of the nuclear family and a myriad of unresolved personal and spiritual conflicts have given rise to a growth in psychological studies and a corresponding decline in discipleship ministries. I believe the ministries of counseling and discipleship are essentially the same in the Bible, but they have become two distinct disciplines with different curricula taught in different departments in Bible schools and seminaries.

Graduate and undergraduate degree programs in psychology have experienced tremendous growth in Christian colleges and seminaries. This proliferation of psychology has greatly influenced the church. This trend has led some pastoral leaders to be antipsychology, which is unfortunate. By definition, psychology is a study of the soul and theology is a study of God. The problem is, secular psychology makes sense if all you are doing is studying the flesh patterns of fallen humanity, explaining their pathology and helping them cope. The Bible clearly defines the nature of our soul, why we are here, and how we can be complete in Christ. Committed Christians should question a secular psychology as they would question a liberal theology, but they should thirst for a biblical understanding of who we are as new creations in Christ.

The Christian contribution is marginalized when secular psychology labels flesh patterns that have no biblically equivalent terms. Psychological labels are a categorization of symptoms, which are essentially patterns of the flesh. Labeling establishes no causation or suggests any sure remedy. Faith and repentance are seldom considered, and they are the means by which we relate to God. What seems to be lacking is a theology of resolution, which is impossible without Christ.

As Christian pastors, counselors, and disciplers, we have a gospel. We can't fix anyone's past, but we can help the children of God be free from it. The apostle Paul wrote, "It was for freedom that Christ set us free" (Galatians 5:1), but how many are living like children of God and experiencing a liberated life in Christ? The defeated or struggling Christians I have had the privilege to work with all had one thing in common. They didn't know who they were in Christ, nor did they understand what being children of God really meant. They were ignorant or confused about their spiritual heritage (see Ephesians 1:18-19). If the Holy Spirit is bearing witness with our spirit that we are children of God (Romans 8:16), why aren't they sensing it?

Connecting People to God

Knowing who we are in Christ has a profound effect on Christian recovery ministries. We are not sex addicts, alcoholics, and drug addicts, or co-addicts and codependents. We are children of God who struggle with certain flesh patterns, but those flesh patterns do not determine who we are. It is not what we do that determines who we are. As new creations in Christ it is who we are that should determine what we do. The Holy Spirit testifies that we are children of God, convicts us of our sins, leads us into all truth. Our response is to live by faith according to what God says is true and to walk by the Spirit. Then we will not carry out the desires of the flesh (Galatians 5:16).

Secular programs will encourage you to "work the program because the program works." There isn't any program that can set one free—only Christ can do that. If Christ is the central focus then almost any program will work. If Christ isn't the focus, then no program will be lastingly effective no matter how biblical it appears. However, if connecting people to God through genuine repentance and faith is the focus, then a biblical program that is good and balanced will bear more fruit than one that isn't.

The Christian counselor/discipler is aware of God's presence and knows there is a role that God and only God can play in the other person's life. Only God can heal the brokenhearted and set the captive free, and He is present in every counseling session whether He is acknowledged or not. God's role is an integral part of the discipleship counseling process, and the Holy Spirit discloses God's presence to the person who is being counseled and leads them into all truth, which sets them free. When personal and spiritual conflicts are resolved through genuine repentance and faith in God, believers sense their new life in Christ.

Dr. Fernando Garzon conducted research applying the principles of discipleship counseling to therapy.* Dr. Garzon gave a number of reasons why this approach is so effective. It...

1. clearly connects the client's faith with the healing process

2. establishes the client's identity and sense of worth in Christ

3. deepens the client's faith commitment

4. clearly connects the Word of God itself with healing and restoration

---

* Neil T. Anderson, *Discipleship Counseling* (Ventura, CA: Regal Books, 2003). Case studies and results are given in Neil T. Anderson, Fernando Garzon, and Judith King, *Released from Bondage* (Nashville, TN: Thomas Nelson, 2002). In regard to the following points, see pp. 142-146.

5. increases personal responsibility in the healing process

6. empowers the client

7. strengthens object constancy

8. speeds up awareness of defense mechanisms

9. shortens the uncovering process

10. confronts the past

Resolving Personal and Spiritual Conflicts

In many Christian circles there are abundant opportunities to grow in our faith, but few opportunities to seek personal help for resolving personal and spiritual conflicts through genuine repentance and faith in God. Christians will never experience their new life and freedom in Christ without repentance. *Repentance* literally means a change of mind, which resonates with cognitive therapy. Cognitive therapy is based on the belief that people are doing what they are doing and feeling what they are feeling because of what they have chosen to think or believe. Therefore, we should seek to help people assess what they are thinking and believing.

However, for cognitive therapy to be effective the following must be taken into consideration:

1. Even if cognitive therapy is practiced consistently with the Word of God, it is not enough without the life of Christ. Cognitive therapy can change how people feel and behave, but they cannot change who they are without Christ. Therefore, we must help Christians be reconciled to God so that the life of Christ will be manifested in their lives. Connecting people to God gives them power to change.

2. Effective Christian counseling requires a biblical worldview, which includes the reality of the spiritual world. "The Spirit clearly says that in later times some will

abandon the faith and follow deceiving spirits and things taught by demons" (1 Timothy 4:1), which is happening all over the world. Much of what is believed to be mental illness is in reality a spiritual battle for the mind. Nearly all those hearing "voices" or struggling with blasphemous and condemning thoughts are set free when they submit to God and resist the devil (James 4:7). The natural tendency is to polarize into psychotherapeutic ministries that ignore the reality of the spiritual world or some kind of "deliverance" ministry that ignores psychological problems and personal responsibility. We are empowered and led by a whole God, who deals with the whole person, who takes into account all of reality all of the time. It is His children we are endeavoring to help, not "my" clients or "my" people.

3. Jesus is the Wonderful Counselor and the Great Physician, and He alone grants repentance leading to a knowledge of the truth (2 Timothy 2:24-26). I respect the fact that some have pointed out that our limited human role is to *care* for the soul, but if God wants to *cure* the soul, then why are we excluding Him from counseling and discipling ministries? Discipleship is the process of building into one another the life of Christ, and so is Christian counseling. We don't have the power to change anyone but ourselves, but God does—and that is part of the sanctification process. Ultimately, apart from Christ we can do nothing, but why settle for that? It is the eternal purpose of God to make His wisdom known through the church (Ephesians 3:10), and He has limited Himself to work though us as we endeavor to help others during this church age.

Discovering who we are in Christ, understanding the reality of the spiritual world, and incorporating Christ in the ministry process were life-changing and fruit-bearing experiences for me, but the biggest change took place when I started to understand how prayer is effective in the repentance process.* When working with people, I would inevitably get stuck and not know what to do next. I believed Christ was the answer and truth would set them free, but I didn't know how—and I would tell them so. I would stop and pray, asking God for wisdom.

The Prayers of Repentant Hearts

One day I realized I was asking God to tell me so I could tell those I was helping. That made me a medium, and there is only one intermediary between God and humanity. The apostle Paul wrote, "There is one God and one mediator between God and men, the man Christ Jesus" (1 Timothy 2:5). That is why we have inquirers pray as they go through the Steps. Then God brings them the conviction and guidance they need. This brings them into direct contact with their heavenly Father. To illustrate, suppose you had two sons, and the younger son was always asking his older brother to ask you for money or favors. Would you accept that? Neither does God, and I don't either. We can't have a secondhand relationship with God, and it is our ministry to help them have a personal one.

I started to have the person I was working with pray and ask God who they needed to forgive, and how they had sinned and been led astray. This led to the Steps to Freedom in Christ, which is a discipleship counseling tool being used all over the world. James wrote, "Is any one of you in trouble? He should pray...Is any one of you sick? He should call the elders" (5:13-14). We will never see wholeness and victory in Christ until we help believers be reconciled to God and assume responsibility for their own attitudes and actions. If you want to be effective in discipling and counseling others, then you should help struggling Christians discover who they are in Christ, connect them to God through faith and repentance, and watch the Wonderful

---

* See Neil T. Anderson, *Praying by the Power of the Spirit* (Eugene, OR: Harvest House, 2003).

Counselor set His captives free and heal their wounds right before your eyes.

The obvious problems volunteered by inquirers are symptomatic in most cases. They are not the root causes, and they usually represent only a portion of the issues that are important between them and their heavenly Father. God will convict us of our sins, grant repentance, and lead us into all truth that will set us free.

Suppose an inquirer presents a problem between himself or herself and another family member. The pastor or counselor may discern some bitterness on the part of the inquirer and encourage him or her to forgive that family member. That is appropriate, but it's not enough. As they go through the Steps, God will bring to the surface another group of names of others the person needs to forgive as well, and will also reveal false guidance, deception, pride, rebellion, sin, and iniquities passed on from previous generations. Most of those issues would never show up in typical counseling sessions, but they are very important issues in terms of a person's relationship with God, and He perfectly knows what they are.

A Wholistic Answer

That is why we should never think of people as having one particular problem, such as sex. Treating their sexual addiction will never be enough to bring about complete resolution and freedom. There is never a single diagnosis. Anybody that has an addictive problem to anything is likely to be struggling with a poor sense of worth, anxiety depression, fear, anger, bitterness, and so on. Those issues are not resolved by abstinence. Just trying to help people stop drinking, using, fornicating, masturbating, gambling, lusting, and so on, doesn't work.

The goal is to help them genuinely repent and get back into a righteous relationship with God. If you are prideful, God is opposed to you. If you are bitter, He will turn you over to the tormentors. I have never yet taken anyone through the Steps to Freedom who hasn't had someone—and usually many people—they need to forgive. That is especially true for those who have sexual problems. If you are rebellious, that is the sin of divination. If you have sought false guidance and dabbled in the occult, the devil will take advantage of it. If you have sexually used your body as an instrument of unrighteousness, you have allowed sin to reign in your mortal body.

Taking someone through the Steps is a ministry of reconciliation, which removes the barriers to their intimacy with God. Christ is the answer, and truth will set them free, and the ministry of the church is help people get back into a righteous relationship with God. When we include God in the process, we never have to point out their sins. God does that. We just encourage them as they go through the process. This process brings the darkest part of the inquirer's life to the surface, and they are grateful for it. It leads to repentance without regret (2 Corinthians 7:9-10).

We will never see wholeness, freedom, victory, and genuine growth in God's children unless we help them understand what is essentially their responsibility. We cannot think for inquirers, confess for them, believe for them, repent for them, or forgive others for them, but we can help them. Discipleship counseling empowers believers to determine their own destiny. If they refuse to accept responsibility for their own attitudes and actions, there is not much anyone can do for them. Our prayers become effective for others after they have confessed their sins and gotten right with God. As encouragers, however, we do have a role to play, as 2 Timothy 2:24-26 shows:

> The Lord's bond-servant must not be quarrelsome, but be kind to all, able to teach, patient when wronged, with gentleness correcting those who are in opposition, if perhaps God may grant them repentance leading to the knowledge of the truth, and they may come to their senses and escape from the snare of the devil, having been held captive by him to do his will.

Effective Christian discipler/counselors are first and foremost bondservants of God, which means they are dependent upon Him. They do not lean on their own understanding, but in all ways they acknowledge Him. They practice the presence of God and try not to usurp His role in the lives of one of His children. God is the One who grants repentance, leads His children into all truth, and sets them free. The Steps to Freedom in Christ don't set anyone free. Who sets them free is Christ, and what sets them free is dependent upon what they choose to believe and repent of.

At a denominational meeting, a pastor handed me a card that said, "You've been His salt in my life." I didn't know this pastor, and I don't think he has taken our discipleship counseling training. In the card he wrote,

The card is true. God has used you in my life, my marriage, and my ministry. I do thank the Lord and you for the materials you have created. It is wonderful to use something that works with all sorts of people with all sorts of problems.

> I stumbled onto your material a year ago. I used it for Sunday school, and God used it to prepare us for working with a severely demonized man. In preparing for the Steps with him, the elders and I went through the Steps first. I personally had the bondage to sin broken in my life, which was lust and masturbation that started as a child with looking at my dad's *Playboy* magazines. As a result of it, my wife found freedom from her family's occultic background.

> I'm in a new church now. Not much happened in the first two months, but without advertising or promoting, God has sent over 12 people to me in January to go through the Steps. There has been a great work of God in people's hearts. Two elders resigned to get their lives straightened out. One has been having an affair for the last two years. He told me that his hypocrisy didn't bother him until I came. It was the Lord! Not me! I'm honored that God utilized me to touch lives. I'm taking him and his wife through the Steps this next week.

> I took the other elder and his wife through the Steps last week. He had bondage to pornography, masturbation, and strip joints when he was on business trips. It was wonderful to see both find their freedom, and renew and deepen their

relationship. What a joy and privilege to encourage people as they go through the Steps.

One of our Sunday school teachers has been experiencing night-time terror and demonic dreams. Through God's "chance events," she told my wife about these difficulties. I took her and her husband through the Steps two weeks ago. When we came to forgiveness, I had to teach, exhort, and encourage her for over an hour. I had to physically put the pencil in her hand to write down the names God was revealing to her. It took her 30 minutes to write down the first name. But eventually she made a decision and went for it! God is so good! The next Sunday there was so much joy, peace, and freedom on the face of both her husband and her.

It is a joy to see people's lives change—to see them personally feel the freedom and enjoy their relationship with their heavenly Father.

FOLLOW-UP

Going through the Steps to Freedom in Christ is not an end. It is a beginning. For many, the book entitled *Restored* would be very helpful.* It expands and illustrates the Steps and provides inquirers an opportunity to reinforce the decisions they have made. Some will not be able to go through the Steps on their own. Usually this is due to major abuse or their involvement in the occult. They will need someone to guide them through the process and help them maintain their objectivity. The book *Discipleship Counseling* will give the needed additional instruction and provide the biblical basis for this ministry.

Those who have found their identity and freedom in Christ still have to deal with their flesh patterns. There is no such thing as instant maturity. However, their ability to read the Bible and process biblical material will be greatly enhanced. Those seeking treatment for addictive behaviors will be far more successful if they have good Christian fellowship and an accountability group.

---

* Neil T. Anderson, *Restored* (Franklin, TN: e3 Resources, 2007).

Notes

1. According to an editorial by Pulitzer prize-winning cartoonist Steve Benson in the June 24, 2003, edition of the *Arizona Republic*. He further stated, "The battle is over, the gays have won." One would have to agree that he is at least partly right when you read an August 6, 2003, article from the same newspaper which reported that the Episcopal Church of the USA had confirmed its first openly homosexual bishop, Gene Robinson, who had previously left his wife and family to live with another man.

2. "The Best Research Yet," Stanton Jones and Mark Yarhouse, *Christianity Today*, October 2007, p. 52.

3. Centers for Disease Control and Prevention, "Tracking the Hidden Epidemics: Trends in STDs in the United States" (2000), p.1. Accessed via Internet at www.cdc.gov/nchstp/dstd/Stats_Trends/Trends2000.pdf.

4. S.J. De Vries, "Sinners," G. Buttrick et al., *Interpreter's Dictionary of the Bible*, vol. 4 (Nashville, TN: Abingdon Press, 1962), p. 365.

5. De Vries, p. 366. De Vries comes to his conclusion based on the following:

   "The corporate involvement of sin deeply impressed itself upon the people...The prophets proclaimed that it was not only a few wicked individuals, but the whole nation, that was laden with sin (see Isaiah 1:4). Generation upon generation treasured up wrath. Thus it was easy for those who were finally forced to bear the painful consequences to protest that all the effects of corporate guilt were being visited upon them. The exiles lamented: 'Our fathers sinned, and are no more; it is we who have borne their iniquities' (Lamentations 5:7). They even had a proverb: 'The fathers have eaten sour grapes, and the children's teeth are set on edge.' Against this both Jeremiah and Ezekiel protested (see Jeremiah 31:29-30; Ezekiel 18; 33:10-20). No son was to be held accountable for his father's crimes. 'The soul that sins shall die' (Ezekiel 18:4)." (De Vries, pp. 365-366).

6. Maxine Hancock and Karen Burton-Mains, *Child Sexual Abuse: A Hope For Healing* (Wheaton, IL: Harold Shaw Publishers, 1987), p. 12.

7. Herant A. Katchadourian and Donald T. Lunde, *Fundamentals of Human Sexuality*, third ed. (New York: Holt, Rinehart, and Winston Publishers, 1987), p. 379.

8. Adapted from Neil T. Anderson, *The Bondage Breaker* (Eugene, OR: Harvest House Publishers, 2000), pp. 53-57.

About Dr. Neil T. Anderson

Dr. Neil T. Anderson was a farm boy, sailor, wrestling coach, aerospace engineer, associate pastor, senior pastor, and former chairman of the Practical Theology Department at Talbot School of Theology. In 1989, he founded Freedom in Christ Ministries, which now has staff and offices in various countries around the world. In 2001, Dr. Anderson stepped down as president of Freedom in Christ Ministries and is now on the board of Freedom in Christ Ministries International.

Discipleship Counseling Training

We estimate that 85 percent of the participants in a Living Free in Christ Conference or Beta Course can work through the Steps to Freedom in Christ on their own. The book *Restored* may facilitate that process and increase that percentage. For those who can't work through the process on their own, we offer comprehensive training through books, tapes, and study guides. We encourage churches that use our material to offer this training on a continuous basis.

The material for training encouragers includes books, study guides, and videos. Study guides greatly increase the learning process by helping people personalize and internalize the message. The video series comes with a corresponding syllabus. Trainees receive the most thorough training when they watch the videos, read the books, and complete the study guides. We recommend that the initial training be offered two hours per week for 16 weeks. The material should be presented in the following order:

Basic Training

Sessions 1-4
Video/audio: *Victory over the Darkness*
Reading: *Victory over the Darkness* and study guide

Sessions 5-8
Video/audio: *The Bondage Breaker*
Reading: *The Bondage Breaker* and study guide

Sessions 9-16
Video/audio: *Discipleship Counseling* and *Helping Others Find Freedom in Christ* video training program
Reading: *Discipleship Counseling* and *Released from Bondage*

- *Unleashing God's Power in You* with Dr. Robert Saucy. An analysis of sanctification, along with practical instruction on how you can grow in Christ.

Resources on Specific Issues

- *Getting Anger Under Control* with Rich Miller (Harvest House). Exposes the basis for anger and shows how you can control it.
- *Freedom from Fear* with Rich Miller (Harvest House). Discusses fear, anxiety, and anxiety disorders and reveals how you can be free from them.
- *Daily in Christ* (Harvest House). This popular daily devotional will encourage, motivate, and challenge you to experience the reality of *Christ in you.*
- *Breaking the Bondage of Legalism* with Rich Miller and Paul Travis (Harvest House). An exposure and explanation of legalism, the guilt and shame it brings, and how you can overcome it.
- *Winning the Battle Within* (Harvest House). Exposes bondage in the area of sex and shows you how you can be free in Christ.
- *Who I Am in Christ* (Regal Books). 36 short chapters on who you are in Christ and how He meets your deepest needs.
- *Freedom from Addiction* with Mike and Julia Quarles (Regal Books).
- *One Day at a Time* with Mike and Julia Quarles (Regal Books).
- *Experiencing Christ Together* with Dr. Charles Mylander (Regal Books).
- *The Biblical Guide to Alternative Medicine* with Dr. Michael Jacobson (Regal Books).
- *Extreme Church Makeover* with Dr. Charles Mylander (Regal Books).
- *Christ-Centered Therapy* with Dr. Terry and Julie Zuehlke (Zondervan).
- *Released from Bondage* with Judith King and Dr. Fernando Garzon (Thomas Nelson).

The Victory over the Darkness Series (Regal Books)

- *Overcoming a Negative Self-Image* with Dave Park.
- *Overcoming Addictive Behavior* with Mike Quarles.
- *Overcoming Depression* with Joanne Anderson.

Youth Books

- *The Bondage Breaker® Youth Edition* with Dave Park (Harvest House).

- *Stomping Out the Darkness* with Dave Park (Regal Books).
- *Stomping Out Depression* with Dave Park (Regal Books).

To order the material listed above, please contact the following:

In the USA:

Freedom in Christ Ministries
9051 Executive Park Drive, Suite 503
Knoxville, TN 37923
Telephone: (865) 342-4000
E-mail: info@ficm.org
Web site: www.ficm.org

E-3 Resources
317 Main St., Suite 207
Franklin, TN 37064
Telephone: (888) 354-9411
E-mail: info@e3resources.org

In Canada:

FIC Canada
Box 33115
Regina, SK S4T7X2
Canada
Telephone: (306) 546-2522
E-mail: FreedominChrist@sasktel.net

In the United Kingdom:

Freedom in Christ Ministries UK
P.O. Box 2842
Reading, UK RG29RT
Telephone: (118) 988-8173
E-mail: info@ficm.org.uk

To order youth editions of Dr. Anderson's books coauthored by Dave Park contact:

His Passion Ministries
PO Box 23495
Knoxville, TN 37933-1495
Telephone: (865) 966-1153
E-mail: davepark@tds.net
Web site: www.hispassionministries.com

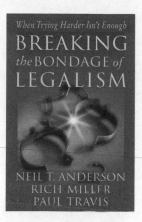

BREAKING THE BONDAGE OF LEGALISM

When Trying Harder Isn't Enough

Neil T. Anderson, Rich Miller, and Paul Travis

> *I was a legalist, a spiritual performer, driven to work hard for God. I had to do right, look right, be right—only then did I believe I would be all right.*
>
> —AUTHOR PAUL TRAVIS

The Bible talks about it. You see others experiencing it—a Christian life that goes beyond fearful, grit-your-teeth obedience...a rich, *joyful* life. Here, in the personal stories of many believers, you'll find encouragement to come home to your Father—the One who longs for your presence and invites you to enter into His deep love. Scriptural insights from the authors will help you understand

- *the bondage that results from legalism:* shame, guilt, pride, a critical and controlling spirit
- *the path of hope and liberation:* knowing who you are in Christ, a true understanding of grace
- *the life you can now live in Him:* joyful intimacy with God your Father and Jesus your Friend

–Includes results from a specially designed Barna Research poll on legalism–

To read a sample chapter from this and other Harvest House books, go to www.harvesthousepublishers.com.